Love Is Now

PETER E. GILLQUIST

Love Is Now

Foreword by Sherwood E. Wirt

ZONDERVAN PUBLISHING HOUSE
Grand Rapids

Love Is Now

To my cherished friend,
Ray Nethery,
whose life is a constant manifestation
of a love that really cares.

Foreword

In May, 1963, when Evangelist Billy Graham came to Paris for a campaign, the French magazine *Arts* devoted several satirical columns to his appearance, titling its report, "La voix de Dieu a l'accent de Minneapolis." Four weeks later the first *Decision* magazine School of Christian Writing opened under the auspices of The Billy Graham Evangelistic Association — in Minneapolis.

In launching the school we did not presume to claim that the voice of God had a Minneapolis accent, but we did venture the hope that out of the annual event would come a band of young, fresh, spirited authors who would speak for God to this generation — in an evangelistic accent. We looked for talented writers who would interpret the saving Gospel of Jesus Christ in the idiom of a new generation.

Among the hundreds of young Christians who have attended the school during the past six years, Peter Gillquist was unforgettable. Tall, blond, Scandinavian, eloquent, Peter brought with him a national reputation as a campus evangelist. For him it was a homecoming, for he holds diplomas from Washburn High School and the University of Minnesota. During our days together God gave him a vision of the power of the printed word to win men.

I am excited about this, Gillquist's first book, not just because it breathes a captivating style, but because it carries the authentic stamp of the man and his tremendous zeal for Christ. The message he proclaims is one to which his contemporaries will respond; of that I have no doubt. It carries the flair and tang of a generation that is trailblazing for the Lord. May God give it a great run, and prove Himself anew to us all.

SHERWOOD ELIOT WIRT

Preface

By all rights, the signature of authorship for this book should be corporate. The theme for its contents emerged from the hearts of five of us — Robert Andrews, Dick Ballew, Jon Braun, Jim Craddock, and myself — who met together over seven o'clock breakfast for fellowship and quest for greater reality in Christ during the summer of 1967. The seeds that God planted within us during those weeks have since sprung up into newness of life for us all, and there is no question whatever in my mind that any of us could have written this manuscript.

We desired the life that God began to show us that summer to be somehow made available to all who would care to share it, not because it was uniquely ours, nor because these truths are often not emphasized, but because through these specific portions of His Word, *our lives were changed.*

To Robert, Dick, Jon, and Jim, I extend my love in Christ, my gratitude for their concern for me, and my thanks for their "life content" which was the basis for this volume. I have borrowed extensively from their experiences, illustrations, and even their very words to attempt to describe the drama of life which God created in us as friends and "soul brothers."

My special thanks to John and Marjorie Dold of Glenview, Illinois, for such unselfish help in the production of the book: to Marjorie for typing and retyping, reading and rereading the manuscript; to John for the long hours he spent in the mechanical duplication of its pages for purposes of editing and publication.

Two men consistently helped me overcome my cold feet which, I suppose, come to most people as they attempt to do anything of major proportion for the first time. These two simply gave me the courage to write: Sherwood Wirt of *Decision* magazine, and Bob DeVries of Zondervan. God used them repeatedly to keep me moving.

Then, there was a person who has never seen this manuscript prior to publication, but who perhaps did more to assist than either I or she will ever know. Her help was vast, yet intangible. She prayed. Mrs. H. S. McIntyre of Minneapolis prayed daily for me as I was writing this book, and to her I extend my warmest appreciation and love in Christ.

In addition to those already mentioned, I wish to thank several others for their helpful and most necessary suggestions in the middle stages of the manuscript: Dean Griffith, Richard Wagner, Dave Sunde, Dick Sawdey, Carroll Anderson, all of the Chicago area, and Terry Thomas of Eugene, Oregon, made constructive comments which formed a pattern to guide final corrections of the copy itself. I tried, whenever possible, to incorporate their suggestions into this text.

My wife and sweetheart, Marilyn, above and beyond her objective observations, provided an "atmosphere" for me from which to write. She was a constant and zealous helper and, as always, was just the one I needed for this particular task.

The closing stages of the preparation of this book leave me with two sensations. First, it is rewarding to be completing this, as with any job. Second, the joy and satisfaction that have been mine in the process of writing the book have been almost without comparison. I have learned much. If these pages reveal but a portion of the love and peace that God has created in my own life to those who read this message, my purpose will have been abundantly met.

PETER E. GILLQUIST

Evanston, Illinois

CONTENTS

Foreword by Dr. Sherwood Eliot Wirt

Preface

Beginnings

For I am confident of this very thing,
that He who began a good work in you
will perfect it until the day of Jesus Christ.

Philippians 1:6

1.

Beginnings

It was springtime; the year was 1959. As we looked across from the east bank, it was good to see the Mississippi flowing again at full force.

The campus itself was coming back to life from its wintry sleep. Weekly rehearsals for Campus Carnival would soon change to three times a week, and finally, every night. The Carnival was a big event at the University of Minnesota, especially if you belonged to a fraternity or sorority.

Things were going too well. There was always plenty to do to keep a person from really facing himself. The Carnival was just a small part of the activity. House parties on the weekends, late-night bull sessions, intramural athletic events. For me, even bad things like grades and classes were no longer a threat. I seemed to have the academic

scene analyzed well enough to at least pull B's and C's —
and what more could a college junior ask for? In addition,
I had just become pinned to a lovely green-eyed blonde,
and was convinced that she was the "one" for me. I was
active on the campus, active in the house and had plenty
of money as a result of two well-paying part-time jobs. My
first car, a spotless 1951 Buick Roadmaster named Charles,
was by far the slickest thing on campus. There was just
one hang-up: no purpose to it all. But why get sidetracked
with peripheral inconsequentials like purpose and meaning
when there is a whole big life to live?

The invasion of this self-erected security shield came
on a Monday evening that spring. It was dinner time and
chapter night which meant all the men in the fraternity
house were together for the evening meeting. Just as we
were finishing dinner, our president announced that we
would be hosting a panel of four men for a half-hour after-
dinner discussion before our chapter meeting began. Then
the bomb was dropped — the subject announced was "Christianity."

My first inclination was to quietly slip out. We had never
had a Christian meeting in my two years as a member of
Sigma Alpha Epsilon, and I, for one, did not wish to begin.
It was not that I was opposed to religion. My thought was,
why flog a dead horse? God and I already had a smooth-
working relationship: I didn't bother Him and He didn't
bother me.

After dinner about seventy of us gathered in the living
room to hear what these men had to say. I had pictured
in my mind's eye four little old fellows with bony index
fingers aimed at me who would get after us for moral mis-
demeanors. They'd be wearing baggy suits, yellowed white
shirts, and have gravy stains on their hand-painted Hawai-

ian neckties. Their eyeglasses would be as thick as the bottoms of Coke bottles, and their beady stares would come through even stronger as a result. I was, without question, psychologically "up" for their presentation!

The first man to speak was an exchange student from India. He was working for his double doctorate at the University. He had come to this country as a Hindu, and his desire, he said, was not just to study in America but also to investigate Christianity. He began by telling us how he had systematically and objectively considered all of the eleven living religions of the world, and had discovered that the founder of just one, namely Jesus of Nazareth, had ever claimed to be God. He studied the life and teachings of Jesus Christ, and terminated his quest by a personal surrender of his life to Him. After his commitment to Christ, he continued, his parents rejected him and ceased to send him monetary aid. For two years he lived by faith, and God met every need he had.

We, listening, were amazed. I doubt that any of us had ever heard anyone talk so intimately of a relationship with God as this young Indian did that evening.

The next person who spoke was not of the same intellectual heritage as the first. In fact, he was the co-captain of our football team. But as he stood and shared with us his relationship to Christ, it was apparent that he, too, possessed the same quality of life as did the first speaker.

By the time the meeting had ended, most of us concluded that either these men had what we wanted, or else they were just plain deluded — one of the two.

A couple of days later I had coffee with one of the men on the panel at the Varsity Cafe on campus. He related in detail how I could experience a true and meaningful walk with God. I knew it made sense, but I felt I needed

time. I asked Ray if he would mind stopping by the house
on Wednesday evenings just so we could talk further. (I
recall that I always invited two or three of the fraternity
brothers to be on hand just so the conversation would not
get too personal.) We began studying the Bible.

It was during the third or fourth week that we had met
together on this basis, that I spotted a passage in the gospel
of John which captured my imagination. Jesus was speaking, and He said, "I am come that they might have life,
and that they might have it more abundantly." [1] The phrase
"more abundantly" was what hit me. Somehow I had sur-
mised that if I were to become a Christian everything
would first have to go all wrong. Then, from the depths
of isolation and fear, I could cry out for my Maker. It is
true that some people come to God that way. I was not
one of them.

Overtly, as I have stated, everything was going extremely
well. Life, I felt, was already abundant. But here was this
thing Jesus had promised in the way of *more* abundance.
Naturally it was appealing. This could well be the answer
to my purpose gap. I told Ray I did not want to be pushed,
but that I was interested. (There was a desire to respond
to God all on my own, so that Ray could not say he had
persuaded me to pray with him.) That night as I climbed
into my top bunk on the second floor dorm of the fraternity,
I pulled the covers over my head and invited Jesus Christ
to enter my life and do with it as He pleased.

I guess I partly trusted in Him as my Saviour, and partly
as my Hero. What spoke to me at that point was not so
much His death for my sins as it was His promise to give
me a better life. I really had no concept of heaven or hell.
A relationship with Jesus was a right now kind of thing.

And I did believe that if I would ask Him to enter into my life He would do it.

The next morning I woke up with a new awareness of His being a part of me. The feeling I had was one I had had before, only far more intense. It's that feeling that usually comes after you do something that you know is right. I sensed that God was pleased, too.

The rest of the spring that year came off as planned. We didn't place in Campus Carnival, but some of the guys did get pinned to some of the girls in the sorority with which we teamed up for the show. The fraternity sponsored a picnic in May, but this time *I* was the one who helped carry a few of the *other* guys into waiting cars when it was over. A new concern for other people, such as I had not experienced since I was a small child, began to express itself.

Of great encouragement was the fact that my pinmate (who is now my beloved wife) had met Christ that same spring, a few weeks ahead of me. I had some catching up to do. Before my turning to God, Marilyn and I had discussed at length her own newly acquired sincerity for going God's way. She was almost bewildered when I received Christ because I had indicated no real interest whatever in the Christian life. After I admitted to her that I had trusted in Christ as my own, we would talk regularly about Him.

In a few weeks school was out, and I was off to Fort Riley, Kansas, for six weeks of military training with the ROTC unit from Minnesota. Letters from Marilyn kept me stoked spiritually, to the point that I began to share with a few of the men at camp my new relationship with Christ.

Back in Minneapolis later in the summer, my thinking began to jell with regard to God's life plan. First, I was deeply impressed by a movie shown at Marilyn's church on the life of Peter Marshall, for it was through this film that God called me as a worker in the body of Christ. Second, at a conference just outside the Twin Cities late in August, I heard a message describing the in-filling of the Holy Spirit, and I felt that through understanding the fact of His life within, my life would never again be the same. A week later, Marilyn and I served as counselors at a church camp in northern Minnesota. As we talked that week with others about knowing Jesus Christ in a personal way, many responded, including some of the other counselors.

I returned to campus in the fall and enrolled for the first quarter of my senior year. The summer had been a good experience. The personalness of the Holy Spirit had become a reality for the first time, and I sensed a new strength and willingness to obey God. From that time on, I never questioned God's presence within me.

But even in the light of what I had learned, things began to go wrong in this matter of being filled with the Holy Spirit. I leaked! Introspection set in, and I began to wonder if little things I was doing would turn Him off. I started to develop a grand capacity to look inward at myself, rather than to look upward toward Christ.

A cardinal point of my personal Christian doctrine at this early stage came over the matter of sin. To me, being filled with the Holy Spirit meant maintaining a spotless fellowship with God into which no sin would come. If I did commit a sin, I felt, my fellowship with Him would be broken, and He would most certainly withdraw His "blessing" and His approval from me. I would carefully confess my sins, but my life itself never seemed to improve that much.

I found myself preoccupied with trying not to sin, instead of depending upon Christ to live within me. There was nothing worse than to tell the Lord in the morning that this day would be His and that I wanted my life completely under His control, and then to have something go haywire later in the day, culminating in hate thoughts or inner anger, and be under the consequences of a total sense of failure for the rest of the day.

The lack of assurance which I possessed regarding forgiveness had nothing to do at all with the things I had done before I was a Christian. I *knew* these were forgiven. The question that arose in my mind again and again was, "What does God do with sins you commit, and even enjoy, after you become His son?"

Answers that came in response to this were varied. They all seemed to have an "if" clause, and the "if" involved would invariably be dependent upon something I must do. Thus, rather than my faith and trust in Jesus Christ increasing, my attention continued to move progressively deeper into my personal spiritual performance.

All this time I was actively relaying the message of Christ to others, especially students, and truly enjoying myself. People were responding to Him with enthusiasm, and in this I found great encouragement.

In order to compensate for the abyss that existed between what I saw in the life of Jesus and what was present in my own experience, I developed an artificial "outside" Christianity. I was subtly moving away from the simple love and trust in Christ with which I had begun, and I tended toward a religious system of performance and duty. When I interacted with people whom I could not love, I learned to speak a vocabulary with inflections that *sounded* like I was concerned. Through sales training in the past, I had learned the importance of eye contact when conversing with others. I developed a way of *looking* like I really cared. Often I did care; other times I did not. People could not tell the difference. With practice, I began to be unaware of this façade myself.

My attitude toward God slipped into a "job centered" relationship. Instead of depending on Him for my life, I began relying upon Him mainly for the tasks I needed to do. For example, from the middle of my senior year in college until the present, I have been asked to give my Christian experience in group meetings. I would pray and ask God to "re-fill" me with the Holy Spirit, and not to let any sin get in my life until the meeting ended. It was like calling up the national guard for an emergency! God, by the way, was always faithful in these times. To me, this demonstrates so vividly His matchless and gracious love.

To perform my Christian tasks I *needed* God. I needed His help because I was convinced then, as I am now, that influencing men spiritually must be done through the Holy Spirit and not through the fleshly strength of the human frame.

For me, and I can see it far more clearly now than I ever did in the past, the key issue was my mix-up on total forgiveness. The problem may have stemmed from back at the beginning of my Christian life when I recognized Jesus more as an example and a standard of life rather than as a Saviour and as my new life itself.

But what happened and what went wrong is not really important to me now. His new life is! And it is this new life which I so eagerly wish to share in the pages that follow.

I am thankful for everything that has occurred both before and after this new understanding on my part of the endless love of God. He has used it all for good. The people whom I have known and with whom I have been associated since becoming a Christian are among the loveliest in God's creation. My experiences with Christ since college have been varied and adventuresome.

But what God has done down inside me—where the human spirit lives—makes me feel like I have been through a spiritual renaissance. God has performed a "happening" for me, and it's still happening. This is no "one day the light dawned" story. God is still unveiling His love and pardon to one who keeps on needing it. It seems I have begun life anew both with Jesus Christ and with my fellow man.

> "And if the beginning be so sweet,
> What must the end of believing be?"[2]

God Is Absent-Minded

He hath not dealt with us after our sins;
nor rewarded us according to our
iniquities. For as the heaven is high above
the earth, so great is his mercy toward
them that fear him. As far as the east is
from the west, so far hath he removed our
transgressions from us.

Psalm   103:10-12

2.

God Is Absent-Minded

Not long ago I was talking with a neighbor. Still on the better side of the generation gap, he is a typical suburban college grad with a wife, two kids and nowhere to go but up.

"I've stopped going to church," he said, almost with a sense of pride. "I'm sick and tired of being chewed out every Sunday and always being told I'm wrong. Don't misunderstand—I don't want to be told I'm a good guy either. I just want something definite; I want a way to really *live*."

He was an easy person with whom to identify. I suggested that he was rejecting a sin-centered message and wanted a forgiveness-centered message instead. With enthusiasm, he agreed.

So much of the typical Christian emphasis today concerns what we _do_ rather than what we *are*. The Church

29

as a whole has become impotent and listless as a result. Instead of getting back to the essentials of what it is that changes a person, many Christian spokesmen are preaching a works-centered, achievement-based, quasi-Christianity. We hear "get involved," "redouble your efforts," "give more," "sin less," "love your neighbor," "why have you not been more faithful?" until we are numb.

Is not what we are doing with this approach treating the symptoms instead of the causes? God's pattern is that works follow faith, not vice versa.[1] But somehow we have developed the mentality that through constant "challenges," people will be motivated to produce and live Christian lives.

The response this message has produced is varied. Among the older people in society there is perhaps the least response. They are neither for nor against the exhortations to achievement. They are just accustomed to them. Among the young set, wide reaction has occurred. How many "second generation Christians" do you know who are deeply responsive to the things of God? There is, I think, a greater tendency on the part of the high school and college-age crowd to reject the message of performance, but not to seriously look again at God to find an alternative. They search elsewhere.

In between these two groups there is a dissatisfaction with Christianity as it is, but also a deeper probing within the Church to come up with some answers. Home discussions, Bible studies, koinonia groups, and similar expressions of renewal are cropping up all across this country.

But regardless of the age group or background, the deadness of the Christian proclamation of today is producing a new concern and a new openness for other avenues of approach. We are looking for a fresh touch from the Spirit of God; for a word which will again ignite a flame of reality and new life within us.

God has spoken such a word. It has been there all along. But it has been lost amid the maze of religious rehash which has blunted the edge of our receptivity to the very life of Christ itself. It is at the point of His forgiving, person-centered love that we will launch our pilgrimage toward the authentic and compelling life which God has promised us.

A NEW SELF-IMAGE

The place God begins in His plan to change our lives is with His forgiveness. The most important element in the Gospel is that in Jesus Christ, God has released us from our sins. Paul said, "For I delivered to you as of first importance what I also received, that Christ died for our sins according to the Scriptures." [2] God says that if you know Jesus Christ in a personal way, every sin you have ever committed — past, present, and future — is totally and completely forgiven.[3] Even the bad ones. Even the sins that may hurt others.

We *think* we understand this, but I do not believe we do! There are certain characteristics that God says will result in the lives of those who are counting on Christ for their forgiveness that simply are not present in the lives of most of us today.

For example, we as believers in Christ possess generally a low image of ourselves. We are down on ourselves, partly because we think God is down on us. We do not see ourselves as forgiven; we see ourselves as not measuring up. We are looking at our actions rather than at Christ. Thus we lack confidence before God. The tendency is to be afraid of Him, rather than to be boldly in love with Him. We see ourselves as having failed.

If we are depending upon Jesus Christ as having cleansed us from our sins, God sees us as perfect. "For by one offering He has perfected for all time those who are sanctified" (Hebrews 10:14). There is nothing that we can do to improve on that which God has declared perfect! And He can say this because through Jesus Christ we have met Him on His terms.

God's ways are so contrary to our ways.[4] We have a hard time understanding His acceptance of us because so much of our orientation in life is achievement-centered. When we were small children, we were told we could have candy *if* we were good. We went to Sunday school and started working for attendance buttons. We joined the scouts and sweated it out for merit badges. In high school, the guys had to make the football team, and the girls tried out for cheerleaders or pom-poms. Senior year came, and some of us took batteries of tests in an attempt to qualify for college. Once we found ourselves in the swirl of campus life, the performance system heightened: Greek life, grades, academic honors, political offices *et alii*. We entered each semester on the basis of how we measured up the semester before, and we had to make it to graduate. If we went right from high school to work, we discovered the fact that we were trying to impress a boss who was trying to impress *his* boss.

Is it any wonder that when God comes along and says He'll take us just as we are that we balk? After all, we've performed for everything we've gained up until this point, and learned long ago that there really is no such thing as free lunch. But God says that Jesus Christ has qualified *for* us and that now we are perfect in Him.

It does something to you to know that someone else thinks you are perfect. It tears down any barriers that might exist. For example, on the person-to-person level, when a man tells his sweetheart she is perfect for him, and she really knows and believes it, her confidence and self-image soar in his presence. She no longer has to be under any pressure at all to prove herself. When a coach tells an athlete he has great ability, his motion becomes all the more fluid. The acceptance by that coach forms a solid base and a certainty from which to operate. And when God says we are perfect in His sight, we are! It removes the pressure from us to give Him a snow job by our lives, and frees us to live authentically by the power of His life within us.

It is a diluted message which says that the cross satisfied God for eternity but not for time. God says we are forgiven *now!* Both for time and for eternity. You are a new person if you are in Christ. Your sins are forever gone. And it is not just your *acts* which are forgiven; *you* are forgiven.[5] God looks at you as being clean. He has remade the real you. You not only have a new, clean suit of clothes, but the person inside is new, too.

Freedom From Guilt

Another huge dilemma for the Christian living under today's "gospel" is this matter of guilt. Guilt is based upon the shortcomings of the past. If we could somehow be removed from what went on before, instead of problems with guilt, we would resound with thanksgiving for forgiveness.

Where there is no assurance of forgiveness, there is no true basis for an unthreatened relationship with God. If we are unaware that He has dealt with our problems of the past, guilt is bound to result. And the problem is complicated all the more when we read in our Bibles that our lives are to be inwardly and outwardly different — and they're not.

In Hebrews 10, a classic on forgiveness, the chapter begins with a summary discussion of the Old Testament sacrificial system and moves very quickly into the application of these truths to the person and work of Jesus Christ. We read in verse two that had the animal sacrifices really worked, "the worshipers, having once been cleansed, would no longer have had consciousness of sins." The implication is almost too good to be true. The following verse says, "But in those sacrifices there is a reminder of sins year by year."

In other words, God is saying that a reminder of sins is just the opposite from not being conscious of sins. In Jesus Christ we need no longer be plagued with a gloom-cloud awareness of our sins.

We know that the Old Testament sacrifice was just a picture of the sacrifice of Jesus which was to come. Since the death of Christ on the cross did satisfy God's demands upon us who were guilty, we can say that His sacrifice "worked." Instead of remembering our sins, as did the Israelites on the Day of Atonement, God wants us to believe they are forgiven and gone, never to haunt us again.

The sacrifices of old were not God's final plan; they were but a picture of the sacrifice of Jesus on the cross which *was* God's final plan of forgiveness. Hebrews 10:12 says, ". . . He, having offered *one* sacrifice for sins for *all time*, sat down at the right hand of God." (Italics mine.) And since His payment was more than sufficient, we need no longer have a consciousness of sin!

Hebrews 10:17 explains why this is true. God says, "And their sins and their lawless deeds I will remember no more." When it comes to our sins, God has forgotten them. He has buried them in the deepest seas.[6] He has separated them as far from us as the East is from the West.[7] They are hidden in the clouds.[8] When it comes to our sins, God is absent-minded!

Guilt is such a screaming thing; forgiveness is so quiet. We often pay more attention to the noise of accusation than to the silence of sins forgiven. And guilt does not come from God. It originates from the lingering accusations of Satan. And we tend to turn our attention to the accuser who condemns rather than to Christ who forgives.

I talk with people who say, "I committed a sin, and I know God has forgiven me, but I still feel guilty." Well, all right, it's a *feeling*. But what is more dependable, the promises of Jesus Christ or the way we feel? Psychologists tell us that feelings are extremely undependable and sometimes even unpredictable. Some mornings I get up and feel no more like a Christian than a jack rabbit! It is *so* important to trust in Jesus Christ rather than in how we feel.

In the early days of aviation, pilots used a descriptive little phrase, "Flying by the seat of your pants." Before instruments were widely available on planes as they are today, the only guide for air navigation in inclement weather was by means of physical sensation. If you felt pressure upon the seat of the aircraft, it probably meant you were ascending, much the same as the feeling you get in a rising elevator. Conversely, if there was a sensation of weightlessness, it most likely meant the plane was on the descent. This means of flying was not at all reliable. Men met their deaths because their feelings played tricks on them.

God has not left us to operate on the basis of human emotion. When He says we are forgiven, He means it, whether we always feel forgiven or not. And He has sent the Holy Spirit to live in our hearts to personally authenticate His promise to us.

While on the Notre Dame campus a couple of years ago, I met a student who had discovered the truth that God forgives and forgets. He used the illustration of a person who had sinned and admitted it to the Lord. Ten minutes later he committed the same sin and muttered, "Oh, God, there I went and did it again." A big booming voice came out of the clouds and said, "Did what?"

That's crude but vivid. God really does willingly forget our sins. He so totally placed them upon His Son that when Jesus died, He took *all* of our sins with Him to the grave. Had He missed one of them, we would be hopeless. James said, "For whoever keeps the whole law and yet stumbles in one point, he has become guilty of all." [9] Jesus had to bear every sin in all the world for the sacrifice to be effectual. And if you have trusted in Him, every sin that you have ever committed or ever will commit is *totally* and *completely* forgiven.

I somehow thought, even as a Christian, that when I died and went to be with God, He would drag out a huge, long list of all my offenses and read it off to me. I assumed I would begin eternity with a deficit balance. God's plan, in antithesis to all of this, is that Jesus paid off my debt and no such list exists. In fact, this is one of the greatest things about becoming a Christian. God not only wipes the slate clean, He also throws the slate away. We pass from death into life. "There is therefore now no condemnation for those who are in Christ Jesus." [10] We are released from our sins.

The question may come to mind. "If God forgets all my sins, what on earth is it about me that He remembers?"

"For God is not unjust so as to forget your work and the

love which you have shown toward His name, in having ministered and in still ministering to the saints." [11]

What is it that God recalls about you and me for all eternity? Our good works. The things that result in our lives because we are trusting Him. Thus, our identity with Him is no longer one of condemnation, but one of commendation. He has forgotten our evil deeds of sin and rebellion and sees us as clothed in the righteousness of Jesus Christ.

A New Awareness of Life

Now here's the exciting thing: if God has forgotten my sins, I can forget them too. The barrier does not exist between God and me any more. That's what it means to no longer have a consciousness of sin: to see our sins as God sees them: judged, paid for, buried, and gone.

So often our attention is focused on our sin and its badness, rather than on Christ and His goodness. We live, in effect, sin-centered lives instead of Christ-centered lives. Somehow we become convinced that holiness involves trying not to sin. God, on the other hand, frees us to forget our sins and depend upon Jesus Christ for our righteousness.

Suppose I get out of bed in the morning and think to myself, "All right, your three biggest sins are temper, lust, and criticism of other people. Today, I will not become angry, I will not lust, and I will not criticize others. And, God, I want You to help me." By setting up a list of "don'ts," I am already indulging in them.

It's like going on a diet and making a mental list of the twelve things you can't eat. You read in your Bible that your body is the temple of the Holy Spirit, and you plainly do not want a fat temple! So with your list of prohibitions in mind, you walk through the cafeteria line. And guess what you crave more than anything else—that which you cannot have. Trying not to sin makes us sin more. God says forget it. What a difference! In essence, my attitude toward sin can be: "Thank You, Lord, that I'm totally and completely forgiven for all my sins. Instead of trying not to sin today, I'm just going to trust You. Thanks for setting me free, Father, to receive the life You are producing within me."

Put this book down for a moment and picture in your mind a red-faced monkey. Got it? Now, the moment you finish reading this sentence, erase from your mind the image of the red-faced monkey. Doesn't work, does it? I am alarmed when I think of how we do the same thing with sin! Instead of believing that sin is covered through the blood of Christ, we resurrect it again from the dead. God is satisfied by the Lord Jesus, and we can add nothing on our own to increase His satisfaction.

It is interesting that the Apostle Peter picks up this same truth in his second letter. As he begins the book the thesis of his first chapter is growth in the Christian life. He starts out by reminding his readers that all things have been given to them pertaining to life and godliness. Then he admonishes them to add to their faith moral excellence, knowledge, self-control, perseverance, godliness, brotherly kindness and finally godly love. He says that if these qualities are in their lives and are on the increase, they will be fruitful in their walk with God. He then tells them why it is that they aren't growing as they ought: "For he who lacks these qualities is blind or shortsighted, having forgotten his purification from his former sins." [12]

What is God's analysis of the problem of stunted spiritual growth and development? It's clearly not our failure to go to church, have devotions, think clean thoughts, and all our other Christian solutions. Our problem is that *we've forgotten we're forgiven.* We've failed to remember that Jesus was not kidding when He said, "Your sins have been forgiven." [13]

When we are trusting Jesus Christ, life — His life within us — is the beautiful by-product. What is more real to you right now: your failures so far this day or Jesus Christ? If it's the former, don't worry; you're forgiven! The solution for the failure? Faith. Trust. Relying on Him. *He* sees *you* as already complete, possessing the very life of God on high.

Portraits of Forgiveness

...It does not depend on the man who wills or the man who runs, but on God who has mercy.

Romans 9:16

3.

Portraits of
Forgiveness

When our first child, Wendy Jo, was four years old, God taught us a beautiful lesson through her. It was after dinner and her mother had just put her to bed. At that time, we lived in a rather small, two-bedroom apartment. Often Marilyn would put Wendy to bed in our bedroom, and the other children in the nursery, to help keep them from talking with each other while they were supposed to be asleep.

Marilyn was out in the kitchen finishing the dishes when she heard Wendy jumping on our bed. She walked back to our bedroom and told her to quiet down. A few minutes later, the jumping resumed. This time the instruction was much more specific. "If I have to tell you again," Marilyn told Wendy, "you will get a spanking. Besides, Mommy's favorite lamp is on the table next to the bed, and I'd feel terrible if anything were to happen to it. Now be quiet and go to sleep."

The lamp on our bedside table was one of the prettiest we had ever seen, and just right for the room. It had come from a large, stately home on the North Shore in the beauiful Chicago suburb of Winnetka. We were always sure to have it aglow when guests came to call.

Back in the kitchen for the third time, Marilyn thought she heard the sound of a bouncing child. Just before she reached the bedroom there was a distinct crash.

After the execution of the spanking, Marilyn took Wendy in her arms, hugged her, and said, "The reason I spanked you was because you bounced on the bed after I told you not to." Marilyn then proceeded to sweep up the remains of the shattered lamp. Wendy watched with dismay. When all the pieces were removed from the floor and the lamp was solemnly discarded in the trash box, Marilyn told her, "As far as the lamp is concerned, Mommy loves you and forgives you, and I'll never mention it to you again."

The next day Marilyn was walking through the apartment and inadvertently stepped on one of Wendy's toys and smashed it. She felt terrible. Wendy ran over and picked it up and said, "Mommy, I forgive you for that, and I'll never ever mention it to you again."

What a portrait of forgiveness! When we really grasp it, our lives are changed without self effort. That is why forgiveness is a proof of God's love.[1] We know we are loved because we know we are forgiven. God wants us to see ourselves as totally forgiven, just the way He sees us. His forgiveness affects not only our understanding of His love for us, but it affects the love we show for ourselves, for others (as was the case with Wendy Jo), and for God Himself. *Our view of forgiveness really determines our love for God.*

Jesus had been invited to dine with a Pharisee named Simon.[2] During the meal, the intimate party was interrupted by a woman of the street, a prostitute. For no apparent reason, she walked up behind the Lord, and weeping, she began to wet His feet with her tears. Then she wiped them with her hair, kissed them, and anointed them with perfume. Simon the Pharisee was angry. His plans for the evening were in jeopardy.

"This woman is ruining my dinner party," he no doubt thought to himself. "Here's my chance to make some points with the Lord, and she is ruining the whole affair. Besides, if Jesus were all that much of a prophet, He'd spot her for what she is, a real loser."

Just then Jesus spoke up. Let's join the Biblical text:

> "Simon, I have something to say to you." And he replied, "Say it, Teacher." "A certain money-lender had two debtors: one owed him five hundred denarii, and the other fifty. When they were unable to repay, he graciously forgave them both. Which of them therefore will love him more?"[3]

Now Simon was probably shrewd when it came to business deals. It was no secret to anyone that he had some denarii signs in his eyes. Jesus was speaking his language. Simon caught the point and came up with the right answer. "The one who got off the hook for the greater amount," he said.

It is here that the grace of the Lord Jesus Christ really comes through. Here was Simon who, as a Pharisee, knew all the right answers, but he didn't know the right questions. The woman, on the other hand, had some questions, but was short on answers. In fact she was low on questions too. But she knew that Jesus had a quality of life that was foreign to her own experience. In place of asking Him questions, she simply showed up at the dinner and tried to convey her feelings for Him as best she could. The Biblical text does not record one word she said. Jesus knows men's hearts. ". . . Man looketh on the outward appearance, but the Lord looketh on the heart."[4] The desire of her heart toward Him was far greater than that of Simon. Jesus took her as she was.

> And turning toward the woman, He said to Simon, "Do you see this woman? I entered your house; you gave Me no water for My feet, but she has wet My feet with her tears, and wiped them with her hair. You gave Me no kiss; but she, since the time I came in, has not ceased to kiss My feet. You did not anoint My head with oil, but she anointed My feet with perfume."[5]

Here were three major customs of the day: the washing of feet, a kiss of greeting, and the anointing of the head with oil. Instead of washing His feet, she cried on them; instead of giving Him the kiss of greeting in the customary fashion on the cheek, she kissed His feet; and instead of anointing His head with oil, she poured perfume on His feet. And the Book of Proverbs suggests that perfume in those days was a mark of the trade of a prostitute.[6] She did everything wrong, but she tried her best to show she loved Him. She somehow must have had the assurance that here was One who could help meet her deepest needs.

Jesus, still addressing Himself to Simon, said, "For this reason I say to you, her sins, which are many, have been forgiven, for she loved much, but he who is forgiven little, loves little."[7]

If we know we are totally forgiven, loving God will come as a natural result. If we, on the other hand, see God as having only partly forgiven our sins, we'll have a tough time loving Him. Our attention will be back on our sins rather than upon Christ and His forgiveness. And the conclusion we will inevitably draw is that God is pleased by our not sinning rather than by Jesus' sacrifice for us. This was, in essence, Simon's problem. A program of good works to gain God's favor, not faith, was the result. This is not to say that God condones sin. But it is to say that He desires for us to agree with Him that we are forgiven, that Christ is presenting us faultless before Him, so that our eyes will be taken off our sins and turned toward Him. Holiness comes neither by trying to be good nor by trying not to be bad. It comes through depending upon what God says we already are in Jesus Christ, and through relying upon Him to remake us into His image through the Holy Spirit.

I had just finished speaking to an exciting group of college students in a fraternity living room at the University of Iowa when a girl came up and said she wanted to talk. "I really like what you said tonight about forgiveness," she said, "but I just can't seem to get it in terms of my experience. I know when I sin, and I know I'm wrong when I do it, but I still keep right on living in my rut."

We sat down and began to talk, and I inquired about her background. "When did you come to know Christ?" I asked.

"It was when I was nine," she responded. "I was baptized at that time. But I still don't understand what it means to be forgiven. You say that when you really count on your forgiveness, you find life changing, and I'm not seeing mine changed at all."

During the next twenty minutes or so, we went through every major passage with which I was familiar in the New Testament on the subject of forgiveness. We talked about the fact that God sees us as perfect in Christ, that He not only forgives, but also forgets our sins. We discussed the importance of remembering our forgiveness if we do sin. Still the haze refused to lift. She just did not get the picture. In fact, it was as though we were conversing about two entirely different subjects, she one and I another.

Finally, I said, "If you promise not to get angry, I'll tell you what I think your problem is."

"What's that?" she asked.

"You're not really a Christian," I replied, expecting the worst.

"I was afraid of that," she admitted. "Christ never has been real to me."

We prayed together, and with gratefulness she invited Jesus to enter her heart and life. She thanked Him for cleansing her from everything in her past, her present, her future. After we finished praying, we talked for a few minutes more. Then, spying a friend across the room, she rushed over to tell her what had happened — that she now had a personal relationship with Jesus Christ. On her way out the door, she turned to say good-by. Her last words before she left were, "I *know* that I'm forgiven."

Forgiveness is the starting point of our faith. I am convinced that if more people knew from the initial moments of their life with Christ that their sins were no longer an issue, we would see far fewer problems in Christians' lives. Man needs to know he can be made new! Medical reports tell us that something like fifty percent of the hospital beds in this country are filled with mental patients,[8] and many of them are suffering from guilt. What a tragedy that even many of us who say we know Christ are all "up tight" over our sins, when we should be standing tall in our forgiveness and letting God remake us.

One of the things that has helped me to see more clearly the complete forgiveness that is in the cross of Jesus Christ is to understand more fully the historical pattern from which it was taken. On the Day of Atonement in the Old Testament, forgiveness is portrayed with prophetic clarity. The story and its applications are found in Hebrews 9.

The Tabernacle of Israel was constructed with two rooms in tandem. The two chambers were separated by a veil. The outer part was called the Holy Place. It was into this section that the priest entered regularly to make the daily sacrifices to God. But the inner tabernacle, the Holy of Holies, was visited only once each year by the high priest on the Day of Atonement. The Holy of Holies was permeated with the glory of God.

Inside the second chamber was the ark of the covenant containing three objects: (1) a golden jar of manna; (2) Aaron's rod which budded; and (3) the tablets of the law. It can be said that these three items together embodied in a symbolic way the sins of mankind. The manna was a picture of man's rejection of God's provisions for him. The rod of Aaron symbolized man's rejection of God's leadership. The tablets of the law illustrated man's rejection of the holiness of God. Across the top of the ark the priest could see what was called the mercy seat, or the place of grace.

Overlooking the mercy seat were two angel-like figures called cherubim, together representing the holy character of God. One stood for the justice of God, which says, in effect, "The soul that sinneth, it shall die," [9] or, "The wages of sin is death." [10] The other cherubim was significant of the righteousness of God, which says, "Be ye holy; for I am holy."[11] God does not grade on the curve; His standards are absolute! This whole scene was a picture of God

looking down upon man and seeing that there was no hope
at all for man through his efforts to enter His presence.
Because of God's righteousness and man's sinfulness, fellowship was hopeless — apart from one thing — forgiveness
on the part of God.

Once each year on the Day of Atonement, the high
priest, having entered the Holy of Holies, would sprinkle
the blood of a spotless animal substitute upon the mercy
seat. During what amounted to 364 days of the year (using the Gregorian year for reasons of simplicity), the cherubim gazed down upon the sins of man and saw him guilty.
On this, the 365th day, the same cherubim would look
down upon the same ark, but this day sin was *covered,*
covered by the blood of an innocent replacement. The
justice of God would see in the blood the death penalty
as having already been paid, and would be satisfied with
the sacrifice. The righteousness of God looked down to
see that it was righteous blood, and therefore saw righteousness instead of sin. Thus, the portrait of the blood sacrifice.

This happened just one day out of the year. But the
Hebrews standing outside the Tabernacle during this event
on the Day of Atonement were fully cognizant of its consequences. As long as that high priest was inside the Holy
of Holies, their sins were being covered by the blood of
a spotless animal. God saw their sins as covered and so
did they. But here's the important thing to understand.
These Hebrews knew that for the amount of time the high
priest was in the inner chamber they were in fellowship
with God. There was no way for the believing child of
Israel to break fellowship with God while the high priest
was still inside. If Christ is our great High Priest, and He
is in the presence of God right this moment in our behalf,
presenting us as perfect before the throne,[12] what does

that say about our fellowship with the Father? Upon what does our fellowship with God depend — the things we do for Him or the things He does for us? Because Christ has come before the holy throne of God for us, if we are trusting in Him and in the authenticity of His sacrifice for us, we are in complete, unbroken, intimate fellowship with the eternal God! There is no way to upgrade a relationship like that. We did nothing to deserve it, nothing to bring it about, and it is for sure we can do nothing to maintain it. That fellowship with our lovely God has been and is being and will be accomplished completely for us by His Son, our personal representative, Jesus Christ. The veil is now gone.

For the Israelite, his "once a year day" was both glad and sad. It was glad, in that all his sins of the past year were covered and declared gone. It was sad because a new scorecard for the ensuing year was put into effect. It would be another year before he could experience this cleansing of the flesh again.

I was speaking at a retreat to a group of students from several Midwestern universities. My topic that particular Saturday afternoon was on the atonement and its foundations in the Old Testament. During my talk, I said, "We as believers in Jesus Christ sometimes take for granted our forgiveness in Him. Can you imagine anything worse than being forgiven only one day a year?" A student in the back of the room, who had just prayed with me the night before to receive Christ, quipped, "Yeah, never having been forgiven at all!"

The Old Testament sacrificial system was the best thing going at the time. I'm sure that when we go to be with God we shall meet Old Testament believers by the droves. But as wonderful as that heritage is, it is nothing when compared to the permanence and the incomprehensible depth of the riches of freedom from sin in the Lamb which God provided,[13] the Lord Jesus. We can echo the words of Micah, "Who is a God like unto thee, that pardoneth iniquity, and passeth by the transgression of the remnant of his heritage? he retaineth not his anger for ever, because he delighteth in mercy." [14]

An Obsession
With Confession

I will bear the indignation of the Lord,
because I have sinned against him, until
he plead my cause, and execute judgment
for me: he will bring me forth to the light,
and I shall behold his righteousness.

Micah 7:9

4.

An Obsession
With Confession

Perhaps by this point the question has arisen in your mind, "Well, if my sins were totally forgiven at the cross — if God really has forgotten them as He says He has — why does the Scripture also tell us to confess our sins?" What is the meaning of First John 1:9 when it exhorts, "If we confess our sins, He is faithful and righteous to forgive us our sins and to cleanse us from all unrighteousness"?

The whole matter of once-for-all forgiveness versus confession arose in my mind shortly after I came to know Christ. I can remember one night in particular when a friend and I struggled with the issue into the early hours of the morning. I had gone east to meet Gordon Walker, who at that time was living in Xenia, Ohio. We started to bat the issue around after returning to our room that

55

night. Admitting that there was no apparent answer to the dilemma, the last thing we agreed upon before falling asleep was, "This must be one of those seeming contradictions which will be answered when we get to heaven."

For years it appeared to me that when we received Christ, all our sins were forgiven and forgotten only up to the point of conversion This was what total forgiveness meant. From that point on, however, the way we *stayed* cleansed was by confession to God on each item of sin. It wasn't so much pleading for forgiveness as it was acknowledging the sin so that He could forgive. But my problem came in (1) keeping the "short account" with God and (2) making sure I caught all my sins in order to acknowledge them. The implication was that if all were not confessed, the guilt for the ones I had missed would keep me temporally estranged from fellowship with God. Any unknown sins, I conveniently thought, would be "automatically" forgiven.

I would meet other Christians for whom sins did not seem to pose that much of a problem. They rarely discussed it. Their conversation revolved around Jesus Christ and the joy that comes from Him. Sin did not seem to enter into their relationship and spoil it. They never appeared to be spiritually "out of it."

One afternoon, another friend, Jon Braun, and I became engrossed in a conversation on the same topic that Gordon Walker and I had mulled over three years earlier. As we were talking in our living room, Jon remarked, "The other day I was in the library taking notes on what I was reading, and First John 1:7 said something to me that I had never been aware of before."

We turned to the passage and I read silently: "But if we walk in the light as He Himself is in the light, we have fellowship with one another, and the blood of Jesus His Son cleanses us from all sin."

"According to that passage, where are you walking when you commit the sin John talks about?" he asked. It took me a few moments to see it because I had never considered a question like that at all. "In the light," I said with great amazement.

"That's the point," Jon said. "The blood of Christ keeps us clean as we walk with Him in the light. That means the monkey is not on our backs to get forgiven, but it's His job to keep us forgiven."

The fog by no means cleared. The confusion was to leave gradually because this was so different from what I had thought until that time. The thing that excited me was realizing that if Jesus Christ would *keep* me clean, there was no reason in all the world why I ever had to be out of fellowship with God again. But what did it mean to walk in the light? Is confession of sin really that important? I still did not see how it all fit together.

WHAT IS THE BACKGROUND OF FIRST JOHN?

Two years and scores of hours of study and interaction centered around the book of First John have followed. I am so enamored by its priceless and simple message of life in Christ that I am convinced it is one of the most important passages in the entire Bible. Its message sets us free from the bondage and depression of sin!

The Apostle John wrote his first epistle right at the end of the first century, in about A.D. 90, partly to help combat an error called "gnosticism" that had crept into the Early Church. The Gnostics taught that Jesus was not really human. They said that Jesus could not be in bodily form and still be God. In line with this, they also denied His preexistence, and taught that God created Him at a point in time. Closely aligned with this error was the Gnostic denial, in a practical sense, of the reality of sin. They maintained the old Greek view of the inherent evil in matter. Thus, that which is material or physical is naturally bad, and that which is non-material or spiritual is naturally good. This not only capsized their view of sin as God sees it, but it also meant that the person of Christ was split into a hopeless dichotomy — the spiritual part of Jesus, which was good, and the material portion of Jesus, which was bad.[1]

With this brief background it is clear why John, in writing his first epistle, began in the manner in which he did.

1. What was from the beginning, what we have heard, what we have seen with our eyes, what we beheld, and our hands handled, concerning the Word of life —
2. and the life was manifested, and we have seen and bear witness and proclaim to you the eternal life, which was with the Father and was manifested to us —
3. what we have seen and heard we proclaim to you also, that you also may have fellowship with us; and indeed our fellowship is with the Father, and with His Son Jesus Christ.

As you read over the above statement describing the life which Jesus presents to us, you will notice John's allusions to the Gnostic problem. He covers the fact that Jesus existed forever, that He was physically observable, and that He is viewed as a totally constituted person — 100% Son of Man and 100% Son of God. In the opening sentence of this letter, John is laying the foundation from which to deal with gnosticism.

Starting in verse 5 John turns his attention to a statement of fact concerning the Gnostics' rather than divine viewpoint of sin. John is the author of contrasts. In fact, the comparison-contrast method of pedagogy was inherent within the whole tradition of the Jewish heritage, of which the apostle was a part. Often the best way to understand a concept is to see it contrasted with something else. And this is the tool that John employs in his writing of First John to help his readers understand. The key to interpreting these early verses in First John is not to see *that* he is comparing and contrasting, but to see *what* he is comparing and contrasting. When we see his contrast, we get a valuable understanding of God's forgiveness from a different perspective.

In First John 1:5 through 10, John begins contrasting two specific kinds of people. To make the distinction live, he borrows two words — darkness and light — from other parts of the New Testament as synonyms for his two categories. Here is what he says:

5. And this is the message which we have heard from Him and announce to you, that God is light, and in Him there is no darkness at all.
6. If we say that we have fellowship with Him and yet walk in the darkness, we lie and do not practice the truth;
7. but if we walk in the light as He Himself is in the light, we have fellowship with one another, and the blood of Jesus His Son cleanses us from all sin.
8. If we say that we have no sin, we are deceiving ourselves, and the truth is not in us.
9. If we confess our sins, He is faithful and righteous to forgive us our sins and to cleanse us from all unrighteousness.
10. If we say that we have not sinned, we make Him a liar, and His word is not in us.

LIGHT AND DARKNESS

The two key words in this particular section of the book, *darkness* and *light,* help characterize the two groups being contrasted and lead to John's usage of the word "confess." There are several New Testament passages which help us clearly ascertain the meaning of light and darkness.

First in Acts 26:18, we have a significant usage of these two words. Paul is quoting from what Jesus said to him during his encounter with Christ on the road to Damascus. Luke records it as follows: ". . . to open their eyes so that they may turn from darkness to light and from the dominion of Satan to God, in order that they may receive forgiveness of sins and an inheritance among those who have been sanctified by faith in Me." Notice that Jesus tells Paul his role in life will be to help turn the Gentiles from one kingdom or dominion to another, that is, from the domain of Satan to the kingdom of God. Darkness is synonymous with Satan's dominion, and light describes the kingdom of God. In God's kingdom there is forgiveness of sins and the promise of an inheritance.

Closely related in content with this Acts passage is First Thessalonians 5:1-6. In these verses Paul is beginning his answer to a question posed by the Thessalonian church regarding the day of the Lord and when it will take place. He starts out by assuring them that even though Christ will come without notice, the suddenness of that day will bring no fear for believers because, ". . . you, brethren, are not in darkness, that the day should overtake you like a thief; for you are all sons of light and sons of day. We are not of night nor of darkness." [3] In this passage the thrust of the Acts 26 impact is enhanced. We see that *all* believers are sons of the light. Christians have no part whatever in the darkness.

In Colossians 1:12, 13, another important reference is made to light and darkness. It is interesting to note that the Book of Colossians was also written to help combat the problem of gnosticism. Here Paul is "giving thanks to the Father, who has qualified us to share in the inheritance of the saints in light. For He delivered us from the domain of darkness, and transferred us to the kingdom of His beloved Son . . . ." It is God through what He does, and not we through what we do, who makes us qualified to be with the saints in light. In pro golf a tournament entrant needs to shoot a qualifying round before he can ever enter the final rounds for the prize money. In the Christian life God shoots the qualifying round for us! In verse 13 both the words "delivered" and "transferred" are in definite past action construction. A parallel passage states: "For you were formerly darkness but now you are light in the Lord . . . ." [2] Our deliverance and transfer from darkness to light is as absolutely accomplished as God could possibly have made it.

Taking this information back into the first epistle of John, it is apparent that the two groups in contrast here are the believers and unbelievers; he is talking about those who are in the light and walking in the light, and those who are in the darkness and walking in the darkness.

In fact, here's an interesting line-up of individual verses in First John 1 and 2 that makes this distinction even more apparent. Read through these verses and ask yourself whether they are describing believers or unbelievers:

> 1:6 If we say that we have fellowship with Him and yet walk in the darkness, we lie and do not practice the truth;
>
> 1:8 If we say that we have no sin, we are deceiving ourselves, and the truth is not in us.

1:10 If we say that we have not sinned, we make Him a liar, and His word is not in us.

2:4 The one who says, "I have come to know Him," and does not keep His commandments, is a liar, and the truth is not in him;

2:9 The one who says he is in the light and yet hates his brother is in the darkness until now.

2:11 But the one who hates his brother is in the darkness and walks in the darkness, and does not know where he is going because the darkness has blinded his eyes.

An Appeal to Know Christ

To say that these passages refer merely to Christians who are out of touch with the Lord seems to me a denial of every other passage in the Scriptures that defines the character of life of a true believer. These, I believe, are unbelieving people, most likely Gnostic in persuasion, which have crept into the church not knowing Jesus Christ at all. John is making an urgent appeal in love for them simply to admit their sins and come to Christ. He is also alerting believers who are under Gnostic influence.

John in this section writes with a style called the "editorial we." By saying "we" instead of "you," he can readily identify with his readers without sounding as though he is preaching at them. (Not a bad example to follow.) Let me paraphrase this section of First John 1:5-10, to show in the language of contemporary life what he is saying:

> Here's the word which we Christians have gotten right from Jesus and are relaying to you, that God is light itself, and if we know Him, we'll be out of the darkness for good. Now if you dear people say that you have fellowship with God, and at the same time walk in the dark, that's double-talk — you're just not telling the truth. But, look, if you want to be part of His kingdom of light, you know what will happen? You'll have fellowship continually with both God and us brothers and sisters, and besides that, the

blood of His Son Jesus will constantly keep on cleansing you from your sins. If you insist on saying you haven't any sin, that's just self-deception and you've been deceived. So here's the key: if you'll just come to God and agree with Him that you've sinned, and agree that He's forgiven you, God is so faithful and so righteous that He will forgive all your sins and cleanse you from every bit of evil within you. But if you keep claiming you have no sin, my friends, you are challenging God and not taking His word for it. You're making Him a liar.

John issued a powerful invitation to trust in Jesus Christ. He told the unbelievers to get with it. I do not mean by this that the entire book was addressed to non-Christians. Not at all. But in his opening remarks John was primarily tuning in on the unenlightened Gnostics and telling them in no uncertain terms the solution that Christ has for their problems. To whom else would he be speaking in language such as this? You don't say to a Christian, "we proclaim to you also, that you may have fellowship with us . . . ." If he knows Christ, the fellowship already exists.

The question comes at this juncture, "If this book is addressed to believers, why would First John 1:9 be there?" I suppose for the same reason that Romans 10:9 is in Romans, Ephesians 2:8, 9 in Ephesians, and Revelation 3: 20 in Revelation. These verses are not *just* for non-Christians, even though they have often been used that way.

Let's take Romans 10:9 for a moment: "that if you confess with your mouth Jesus as Lord, and believe in your heart that God raised Him from the dead, you shall be saved . . . ." The same root word for "confess" is used here as is used in First John 1:9. Now here's the question. According to the Scriptures, how many times does one, in the context of Romans 10:9, need to confess Jesus as Lord to be saved? Little doubt that it's but once. Then does that mean that the person involved, from that point on, never again confesses Jesus as his Lord? Not at all. He has just begun a new life of forthtelling His Lordship. Is this to say, then, that every time he confesses Jesus as Lord he gets "re-saved"? Hardly. A Christian does not confess Jesus as Lord in order to be saved; he confesses Jesus as Lord because he is saved.

WHAT ABOUT FIRST JOHN 1:9?

Now let's look at First John 1:9 in the same context. It says: "If we confess our sins [or literally, "If we are confessing our sins"], He is faithful and righteous to forgive us our sins and to cleanse us from all unrighteousness." How many times does a person need to come to God and confess his sins to be cleansed? One time. Does this mean that you never again agree with God concerning a sin? No. Why would I want to deny that I've sinned? I'm forgiven as it is, so I'm free naturally to agree with God in what He says. That's no problem at all. But does this mean that I get "re-forgiven" if as a Christian I agree with God that something I do is sin? How could that be when everything that needed to be accomplished for forgiveness was done by Christ on the cross? To say that would be to try to crucify Jesus all over again.

The word "confess" means "to agree with God concerning." Concerning what, in this case? First, that it is sin; secondly, that it is forgiven already because God says it is! The passage says we will be cleansed from *all* unrighteousness. How many times can an absolute be repeated?

Not long ago, a man went through a "yield right-of-way" sign, struck our car, and totalled it out. As the wreckage was hauled away, it became clear in my mind that something can only be totaled out one time!

(The reason that I spend this time on First John 1:9 is because I, like so many other believers that I meet, was in introspective knots over the passage. I was constantly wondering if I had confessed all my known sins to God, and if I was in fellowship with God. But the verse says nothing about either being in fellowship or unknown sin. It is dealing with forgiveness and total cleansing, truths that in other passages of the New Testament deal uniquely with the doctrine of salvation.)

God's love for us provides an environment of relationship that is without threat. I have spiritual life within me which engenders trust in Him. Knowing that my oneness with Christ is based with permanence upon His love for me not only produces a new breed of honesty and openness with Him if I do disobey, but it also motivates me to really *want* to do what He says. There is no fear in love.[3] And my attentiveness is turned from its introspective focus on sin to a new and fresh perception of Jesus Christ. There is a different attitude and deeper personal relationship as a result.

Unconditional love on the part of God, and in our own experience, is not to soft-pedal the matter of sin. Love forgives sin, but it does not endorse it. God, in His love, paid an infinite price to forgive us. He did not assume the attitude that boys will be boys, and sweep the whole matter under the rug. Love *gives*. And God gave His only begotten Son to forgive us and release us from our sins. The cost to Him was great.

A Clean Break

God not only *forgives* us, with no strings attached, but He also *keeps* us clean. Earlier in this chapter I spoke of

First John 1:7, which literally says He "constantly keeps on continually cleansing us from sin."

Have you ever had the problem of thinking something evil and then attempting to get rid of it? You say, "Lord, forgive me," and it pops right back into your mind again. So you ask Him to forgive the second thought, and still no results. You don't want to do it. I've been that thought-poppin' route so often I'm sick of it. As I was driving one day from Toledo to Ann Arbor I began feasting on a bad thought. The Lord reminded me that since I was walking in the light as He is in the light, and was having fellowship with Him, that His blood was constantly, completely cleansing me from my sin. What a fantastic truth. It is not up to me to get forgiven, but up to Him to forgive, and He has already done it! As I simply *believed* Him, the thought left. As a matter of fact, I don't even remember what it was. We are forgiven. Why make an effort to get out from under sin when Jesus says it's already gone?

With these things in mind, First John 2:1 and 2 come alive. "My little children, I am writing these things to you that you may not sin. And if anyone sins, we have an Advocate with the Father, Jesus Christ the righteous; and He Himself is the propitiation for our sins; and not for ours only, but also for those of the whole world." It is here that the author turns his letter directly to the believers, the "little children." He says in view of what he has written in the first chapter, we no longer have to sin. Knowing we are forgiven, knowing that Christ is our life, sin is no longer inevitable. It goes back to this thing of not having a consciousness of sin. God wants us to be conscious of our Saviour, not of our sins. He wants us to see sin as a closed case, never to be reopened or reconsidered by Him again.

And God calls Jesus our advocate, or, even more lucid, our defense attorney. He is the One who pleads our case for us.

Picture a courtroom. Jesus is your counsel, you are the defendant, God is the judge, and Satan, the accuser of the brethren, is the prosecuting attorney. You are a believer, and Satan just saw you transgress the law. He says, "Look here, God. Here's your big, holy saint. Here's the person you said was blameless, the justified one, the one robed with righteousness. Look what he just did!"

Jesus immediately steps before the bench and says, "Father, You and I agreed together before the foundations of the world that My death on the cross included this sin as well as all others. Citing the fact I have already paid for it, the sin has been placed on My account, and it is marked 'paid in full.' "

God raps the gavel and says, "Acquitted! Case dismissed. Next case."

In His sight, this courtroom scene took place just once, and you have been awarded the case with finality. You cannot come to trial again. Jesus Christ frees you from the curse, to live in goodness and power.

In First John 2:2 Jesus is the propitiation, or the mercy seat. It is He who covers our sins from the wrath of God. We stand as righteous in Him! We are also told that He is the mercy seat for the whole world. (That is what propitiation means.) God is not even keeping score on the world. All sin was dealt with at Calvary. The only unforgivable sin is unbelief, or rejection of God's sacrifice.[4] The problem is many of us are not counting on His forgiveness, and thus are counting on ourselves. If you are not sure you know Christ, why not at this moment turn from yourself and your inadequacy, and turn to Him as your Lord and Saviour? Tell Him you are relying on Him and His provision for your sins, and that you wish for Him to be your life. Simply thank Him for what He has done in your behalf. Thank Him that He will start you out fresh again in life, making you the kind of person that He wants you to be.

With John, I can say, "I am writing to you . . . because your sins are forgiven you for His name's sake." [5]

Love Is First

The Lord thy God in the midst of thee
is mighty; he will save, he will rejoice
over thee with joy; he will rest in his love,
he will joy over thee with singing.

Zephaniah 3:17

5.

Love Is First

The words "Christian responsibility" come through to me as a misnomer. They generally are employed to describe something I must do if I am going to be a Christian. I would much prefer the term "Christian response." A response is a spontaneous act resulting from a specific stimulus. I "respond" to Jesus Christ, but I tend to get burdened down by thinking I have a "responsibility" toward Him. I mean, how could I possibly, as a mortal being, assert myself as *ever* having fulfilled my responsibility to the God of the universe? It's presumptuous. By allowing me to respond to Him, I feel free, but telling me I have a responsibility to Him makes me feel terribly in bondage.

This is where we need to grab hold of the fact that God's love comes ahead of everything else.

I feel the same way about the word "commitment." I still use it because it has taken on a generic meaning, but I do not like it. In its usual context the word tends to mean that which I do to give myself to God, and it is generally interpreted as being causal in the relationship. We hear the phrase, "You ought to be more committed." Let me ask a question. *How* can I get more committed? What do I *do* to get more committed? If I understand the Word of God correctly, it is not my commitment, but His love, which initiates our oneness with each other.

I am sorry if what I say is bothersome or unnecessary. Maybe I just had to say it for my own benefit, to get it off my chest. But I spend a great portion of my time out among fellow Christians who are doing their absolute best to be "more responsible" and to achieve "greater commitment," and I hurt for them. For me, being responsible or being committed is no longer the issue. The whole concept has been placed in perspective over in the category of "natural responses."

God says that "We love him, because he first loved us." [1] The starting point in our whole identity with Christ is the fact that God loves us. John 3:16 reinforces this truth. "For God so loved the world, that He gave His only begotten Son, that whoever believes in Him should not perish, but have eternal life." God's basic motivation toward us is His love. God loves us first. If He waited around for us to love Him first, He would still be waiting! Love is the first great cause of the universe. God is love. He does not just give love; He is love. Love is the very essence of His being. Because He loves us, a relationship with Him is possible.

A couple of years ago, our family visited Daytona Beach over the Easter break, and I had an exciting time interacting with a few of the thousands of college kids who were on the beach. One evening, it was my good pleasure to meet a young man named Don, a senior at Rutgers University. As we talked, I asked him if he had ever placed his trust in Jesus Christ.

"I could never become a Christian," he said.

"Why not?" I asked.

"Because I'm an agnostic," he answered, just as sincere as he could be.

"Don, God loves the agnostics as much as He loves everybody else," I said.

Now, this sounds pedestrian to most of us, but for him it was music to his ears. He felt that in order to become a Christian he first needed to arrive at the philosophical position of rationally believing in the possibility of Jesus Christ being available to him. I explained to him that God loves us just as we are.

I wish I still had the letter I received from him a few weeks later. He had become a Christian and was engaged to marry a girl he had known for years — a girl who had been praying that he would come to know Christ.

It was the love of God — the realization that God loved him without any qualifications whatever — that drew him to the Saviour.

God initiates His love to us without our ever doing one thing to merit His favor or concern. (In fact, it is quite clear that if we went on the merit system, we would merit His wrath.) In Ephesians 5:22-33 Paul compares the love that God has for us with human marriage. Throughout that entire passage, the husband is told repeatedly to love his wife the same way Christ loves the church and gave Himself for it. The wives, on the other hand, are told to be subject to their husbands as the church is subject to Jesus as its head.

It is interesting to me that nowhere in this exhortation is the wife told to love her husband. The assumption is that she will love her husband as a response to his love for her. He initiates the love relationship; she responds.

In a courtship situation, a man does not seek a woman who will love him; he looks for a woman whom he can love. He is made as the head or the initiator of the love relationship. In a similar way, a woman does not look for a man she can love; she looks for a man to love her. She is created as a responder. And this is what makes a marriage tick. God built the man as the initiator, the wife as the responder, and as he loves her, she, in turn, loves him.

Now, granted, that passage *does* say the wife is to be submissive to her husband. But can you imagine me coming home and saying, "Wife, submit!" That would produce the most awkward and tense situation in the world.

I love my wife, for example, whether the house is immaculate or messy. I don't *demand* dinner at six, or that the kids are bathed and fed. She *wants* to please me because I love her. It is to my love that she responds best, not to my directives. I find that as I simply let Marilyn know that I love her, submission is no problem at all.

Yet, how many of us in our Christian lives picture God standing up in heaven yelling down to us, "Christian, submit!" Our view of God tends to center in His demands rather than in His love. It's difficult to fall in love with an authority figure, but it's easy to love one who loves you. Obviously God has authority over me; He made me. But to prove His love for me, He actually became a man and died for me that I might live. I wouldn't call that pulling authority, would you? He came to us with His love so that we, in turn, could volitionally respond to Him. And His love never wears thin.

The same is true in the human family. One day a friend asked, "Why do you love your kids?" I thought for a minute, and the only answer I could come up with was, "Because they're mine." They need do nothing to prove themselves to me. I take them just as they are. God feels the same way about us. He loves us as we are, and it is His love which motivates us to trust and obey Him in return.

You hear it said quite often in our contemporary world that if we can just become honest with each other, we will be able to identify in vital brotherhood with our fellow man. The thought is that honesty can become the basis of relationship. But honesty comes as the result of love. It is impossible to engender love by simply establishing honesty. I think we all have been in enough "honesty sessions" to discover this. The Scriptures talk about "speaking the truth in love." [2] The truth, apart from love, can become biting and destructive. But where love forms the core of the relationship, honesty is one of the inherent by-products.

Psychologists tell us that man has two basic needs: to love and to be loved. They're right, but their order should be reversed. According to the patterns of Scripture, we first must be loved; then we are capable of loving. The life of Jesus Christ bore the perfect example of this truth. His whole mission was to love us first. During His earthly life, He chose His disciples just as they were and initiated the relationship by love. He availed Himself to the poor and rich alike. Taking no thought for their status in life, He showed His love to them at the point of their need and met them where they were. Even more in His death, He placed His life on the line for a nation that rejected Him and for a race that was oblivious of Him. In Romans we read, "For one will hardly die for a righteous man; though perhaps for the good man someone would dare even to die. But God demonstrates His own love toward us, in that while we were yet sinners, Christ died for us." ³

God loves you as you are right now. He *is* love. If you have been a Christian a million years, and have never done a thing for Him, He still loves you as you are. We do not turn the love of God on and off by what we do. If you have heard the Gospel ten thousand times, and have willingly and angrily turned it down with fervent consistency, He still loves you the same.

It is here that people often ask, "Well, what about hell?" Many of us picture God as being One who delights in choosing up sides, sending some to heaven and some to hell. Somehow the idea has been adopted that everything was going all right up until the time that Jesus visited the earth. But once He arrived, people had to make a choice, and thus the possibility of a life apart from God began to exist because of Christ and what He said.

God is not the One who has changed; it is man. In His love, God formed us and placed us here on earth to have dominion and to walk with Him in fellowship forever. It was man who became the variable and who stepped out on his own. Thus, estrangement occurred. Isaiah wrote, "But your iniquities have separated between you and your God, and your sins have hid his face from you, that he will not hear." ⁴ The separation began when we sinned. And God's love for us was so strong that He provided a way back to this fellowship and dominion we once enjoyed, if we simply wanted it. And the contact point of His love was the cross of Jesus Christ, His Son. The reunion did not come easily for Him. It cost Him His life.

It is interesting that in the Old Testament, the priest on the Day of Atonement had little choice but to enter into the Holy of Holies to perform the sacrifice. Even if no one in all of Israel cared about what he was doing, his motive for sacrifice went beyond them. He had sins of his own. He brought the blood "for himself and for the sins of the people . . . ."[5] Jesus, on the other hand, had no reason whatsoever to die for us, other than that He loved us so much. He had everything to lose and nothing to gain. He had no sin problems at all. His life was laid down *strictly* for our benefit. And if I had been the only one on all the earth to die for, He still would have loved me enough to sacrifice Himself in my stead. It is this, His love, which so greatly motivates me to love Him back, and to allow Him the control and Lordship of my life.

So all of us, apart from Christ, were living in estrangement from God. Hell is simply that estrangement drawn out for all eternity. I have heard people say they are experiencing a hell on earth, and I don't argue with them. What they are really communicating is that they are experiencing separation from God in *this* life. Hell is merely a continuation of that estrangement in the next life. The thing that makes hell hell is not the fire and brimstone, though Jesus made it clear that these elements would exist. Hell is hell primarily because God is not there; it is solitary confinement from Him for ever and ever. And even my natural mind in all its sadistic morbid blackness could never think of anything worse.

Jesus Christ, God's love personified, seeks to rescue us out of this eternal mess. Because of our sin, we are already *in* it. He is not trying to send any more of us to hell; we are all its citizens as it is. His plan is to take all the "whosoever will may come's" out of this godless disarray, that we might be one with Him right now and be fully restored to His eternal purpose. And when people glow over their happiness being as "heaven on earth," it becomes far clearer what they mean. They have passed from death into life, and are enjoying every minute of their restored relationship with Christ.

Jesus loves you right this instant. There is no reason to be afraid of Him or of His will as you trust Him. Perfect love casts out fear.[6] He's *for* you.

Love Is Unconditional

Yea, I have loved thee with an everlasting love: therefore with lovingkindness have I drawn thee.

Jeremiah 31:3

6.

Love Is Unconditional

Because God loved us first, He also loves us unconditionally. God does not say, "I love you if . . . ." He says, "I love you." Period.

In all of secular or religious literature, nothing has ever been penned on the subject of love which even closely rivals God's inspired masterpiece in First Corinthians 13. Men from all ages within the last two millenniums have paid great homage to its peerless expression. Many people read the chapter daily. Evangelist Billy Graham states that it is his favorite passage in the entire Bible.

1. If I speak with the tongues of men and of angels, but do not have love, I have become a noisy gong or a clanging cymbal.
2. And if I have the gift of prophecy, and know all mys-

teries and all knowledge; and if I have all faith, so as
to remove mountains, but do not have love, I am nothing.

3. And if I give all my possessions to feed the poor, and
   if I deliver my body to be burned, but do not have
   love, it profits me nothing.

4. Love is patient, love is kind, and is not jealous; love
   does not brag and is not arrogant,

5. does not act unbecomingly; it does not seek its own,
   is not provoked, does not take into account a wrong
   suffered,

6. does not rejoice in unrighteousness, but rejoices with
   the truth;

7. bears all things, believes all things, hopes all things,
   endures all things.

8. Love never fails; but if there are gifts of prophecy,
   they will be done away; if there are tongues, they will
   cease; if there is knowledge, it will be done away.

9. For we know in part, and we prophesy in part;

10. but when the perfect comes, the partial will be done
    away.

11. When I was a child, I used to speak as a child, think
    as a child, reason as a child; when I became a man,
    I did away with childish things.

12. For now we see in a mirror dimly, but then face to
    face; now I know in part, but then I shall know fully
    just as I also have been fully known.

13. But now abide faith, hope, love, these three; but the
    greatest of these is love.

I can remember hearing sermons on First Corinthians 13
ever since I was old enough to sit still for a half-hour to
listen to a speaker. When the message was concluded, I
would say to myself, "That is correct; I need to love more,"
but nothing ever happened to make me love more. When
I received Jesus Christ into my life, I found a new desire
to love others, and sometimes really did. I was more acutely
aware of my need to love people as they were. But just

how to let go and express the love was difficult. Oftentimes I did not experience love for others, and I knew the answer was in Christ, but I could never seem to get it all the way down from Him to me.

Orations on the theme of love usually took somewhat predictable paths in their intent. The most common challenge was, "You must love others more because it's the Christian thing to do." It was back on the old responsibility kick again. Agreeing that the thesis was correct was no problem; how to perform it in everyday life was. The next most common dimension of application from First Corinthians 13 was, "You and I are incapable of loving others. Therefore, admit your incapacity to God, and let Jesus love others *through* you." That was the route I chose to take.

Either there was something wrong with Jesus Christ or I had a clogged tube somewhere, but whatever it was, there were many people who were not being loved by Christ through me.

Then I heard a slightly different slant on the matter. It isn't so much that He loves other *people* through you, but it is the Christ *in* them which is the object of His love. Now I really felt I'd lost my identity. If He didn't need *me*, but just used me as a channel, and He didn't need other people, except to the extent that they provided free housing for Him, what in the world were we here for? Regardless of what was meant by these reflections on love, none of them seemed to work.

Today I'm so excited about love I can hardly sit still. I sprouted no wings, I have not enrolled for harp lessons, and I have not become sinless. I do not love 100% of the people 100% of the time. But I got locked in with a small group of Christian friends over the course of one summer and learned love — both by experience and through God's Word.

Traditionally we have limited the application of First Corinthians 13 to mean the way we are supposed to love other people. In our consideration of the passage, I would like to use it as a basic description of how *God* loves *you*. And that's valid. Would it be fair, after all, for God to tell you and me to love others in a way He hasn't first loved us? That would make the creature greater than the Creator. And as we have already discussed, God *is* love. Therefore He must love us *at least* as much as love is revealed in that chapter. Let us consider a few portions of that chapter:

Love Is Patient

God is *so* patient toward us. Often we get impatient with ourselves, and the reason we do is that we honestly believe God is impatient with us. But God is extremely patient because love is patient, and God is love. We look at our lives and say to ourselves, "I'm not growing fast enough. I don't do enough for the Lord." Or even, "I don't love Him enough."

How much is enough? There is no *enough*. But He is patient and accepts the love you do give Him. He loves you where you are in your spiritual development. And it is knowing this that frees you to move ahead without the limitations of past performance.

One day I was sitting at my desk when our four-year-old walked through the room trying to thread a needle. If you have never witnessed a small child threading a needle, or attempting to do so, you are in for one of life's great frustrating experiences. The end of the thread was blunt and frazzled, and the needle in her other hand was turned sideways and unsteady in her grasp. My inclination was to snatch it away from her and do it myself. Watching her miss the target over and over again was like listening to a musical number with a dissonant ending; you want to rush to the piano and play the last chord so your soul might rest in peace.

As I watched her, I started to think about the number of times God must want to interrupt what I'm doing and do it Himself. But He is patient. I decided to let her keep trying. Finally, she said, "Daddy, would you do it for me?" I exhaled with satisfaction and relief, took the needle and thread, wet and twisted the thread, inserted it through the needle's eye, and returned it to her. She thanked me and proceeded to play.

Sometimes the Lord lets us get to the end of our rope on a project or ambition because He loves us too much to interfere. If He were to intervene, we would never learn. But once I have tried and failed, and then give it to Him, I know the next time to trust Him with it from the start. God's love is patient, and His patience with me allows me to discover for myself that I can trust Him completely.

Love Is Kind

Kindness is not a personal forte, but God is so kind to me. Kindness means being considerate and not taking advantage of others — not kicking a person when he's down.

Knowing the kindness of our Father has been especially meaningful, for somehow I had acquired the concept of a God who gets even. My view of Him was that as long as I did what I knew was right, fine. But the second I failed, God would not only push the consequences on me, but He would continue to rain dirt upon me until I got back on my feet. The Apostle Paul speaks heavily to me: "Or do you think lightly of the riches of His kindness and forbearance and patience, not knowing that the kindness of God leads you to repentance?"[1]   It is His kindness that encourages me to follow Him whatever the cost.

Here was the prodigal son.[2] He grew up in a fine Jewish home and had everything a person could desire. One day he was doing some elementary math out behind the barn. He figured, "Why wait around till I'm old and wrinkled to latch on to my inheritance, when I could be out living it up while I'm still young enough to enjoy it."

He stopped by the house for his share of the money and took off for town. Soon he was behind on payments on his chariot, owed a bill at the inn, had lost some money on the market, and was out of ready cash. Tragedy of tragedies, he had to go to work for a living. After waiting in line at the local employment office, he finally landed a job slopping garbage to the hogs for a free bed and leftovers from what the swine didn't want. This was Jewish skid row — the idea of being penned in with those unclean beasts! The painful circumstances finally jolted him to his senses, and, after agreeing he was wrong, and willing to make restitution, he headed for home.

Instead of putting his son through the third degree, that father, it says, loved him and "ran and embraced him."[3] He received him with kindness. The lad had learned his lesson. Discipline in this case would have been redundant.

God is not out to get people when they're down. He wants to help them up. Love is kind, and God is love.

LOVE IS NOT PROVOKED

The King James Version of the Bible says, "Love is not *easily* provoked," but the word "easily" is not in the text. God just plain is not provoked; He doesn't get angry. All of the wrath that should have fallen on us came upon the

Lord Jesus Christ. His reason for provocation with us was our sin and unbelief. It was these which Jesus bore. If a person chooses to disbelieve Jesus Christ and strike out on his own, then His sacrifice is made of none effect. The cross dealt with sin, and the price for sin has been paid. The issue for us is not so much good versus evil as it is life versus death. The barrier which kept us from life has been broken down. Jesus said, "Truly, truly, I say to you, he who hears My word, and believes Him who sent Me, has eternal life, and does not come into judgment, but has passed out of death into life."⁴ Therefore, sin is out of the way, and life is our live option.

In Christianity it's not what you know but whom you know. If we reject Jesus, the unique source of satisfaction for the wrath of God, then, by choice, we are stuck with what's left. Wrath is a part of death; love is a part of life. God has done everything He can possibly do to solve our problems of sin and guilt. To quote Jesus, "It is finished."⁵ If we turn Him down, we are saying to Him that we choose to believe it would never work. Thus John was forced to conclude the third chapter of his gospel by saying, "He who believes in the Son has eternal life; but he who does not obey the Son shall not see life, but the wrath of God abides on him."⁶

LOVE DOES NOT TAKE INTO ACCOUNT A WRONG SUFFERED

An account is a list or a ledger, and a wrong suffered is a sin. As of A.D. 33, God deals with neither. Paul said that "God was in Christ reconciling the world to Himself, not counting their trespasses against them . . . ."⁷ God *has dealt* with wrongs suffered, as He promised, and no longer takes them into account.⁸

I was speaking in a church one Sunday and after the

service a woman approached me and said, "How does what you say fit in with the fact that God takes into account every idle word?"

"I'm not sure," I replied. "Let's look it up and see." In thinking through the riches of the grace of God, I had forgotten some of the passages in the gospels that appeared as inconsistencies. We found the passage in question in Matthew 12 and read it in context:

34. You brood of vipers, how can you, being evil, speak what is good? For the mouth speaks out of that which fills the heart.

35. The good man out of his good treasure brings forth what is good; and the evil man out of his evil treasure brings forth what is evil.

36. And I say to you, that every careless word that men shall speak, they shall render account for it in the day of judgment.

37. For by your words you shall be justified, and by your words you shall be condemned.

Jesus was speaking here to a group of men who were vehement in their opposition to Him. They were not believers at all. And as He conversed with them, He made it clear that the only way to speak righteous words was to be righteous on the inside. Idle or careless words are simply evidences of unbelief.

This did two things for me. Negatively, it made me breathe easier over idle words that I had spoken. They were forgiven. Positively, God showed me that because I am indwelt with the life of Christ, righteous words will emerge from me as a result. Consequently, I've found myself having fewer problems with careless words.

LOVE DOES NOT REJOICE IN UNRIGHTEOUSNESS

Several months ago I was riding with a friend through downtown Indianapolis during rush hour. There is no on-the-street parking in the business section of that city from 3–6 p.m. due to the heavy traffic. It was about 3:45. As we were cruising down one of the main streets of town, about two blocks ahead I could see a tow truck back up in front of a huge Mercedes-Benz. The winch slowly lowered, and the driver got out of the truck and came around between the two vehicles to hook them together. About the time we drove past the scene, the car had been hoisted up by the chain, and we could see the truck start up and head down the street behind us.

I howled with laughter. That was one of the most satisfying sights I had seen in years. The reason for my hilarity was that a few years earlier that same thing had happened to me in a *No Parking 4–6* zone in Minneapolis. And it was *so* good to see it happen to somebody else.

That is rejoicing in unrighteousness. God doesn't do that. His source of joy is in the truth. God does not even delight when the devil pushes his own people around. Happiness for God is to see an unbeliever turn to Christ and receive new life. Our Father is so lovely and gracious; He never thinks in terms of evening up the score. He is merciful even to our iniquities![9]

LOVE BELIEVES ALL THINGS

We have been told over and over again to believe in God, and that is as it should be. But God wants us to know that He believes in us. Love believes all things, and God is love.

For years, people told me I did not have the ability to write. One man, with whom I worked, sat me down in his office one afternoon and said to me, "Pete, you just don't have the stuff." I wasn't heartsick over it because whether I could or could not write made little difference to me.

I had some other plans which didn't necessarily include journalism.

Later an editor of a well-known magazine told me that he felt I had some definite potential in the area of writing. A friend in the publishing business actually *encouraged* me to write, and said it with enthusiasm at that. The result is this book.

My purpose in writing is to get a message out. I do not feel I am especially talented in communicating per se. But the fact that a few people believed in me motivated me to get busy.

God really believes in you! He believes that you are a new person, if you have received Christ into your life. He has little confidence in the old you — what you were before you accepted Him — but He knows that you can do all things through Christ, who is your strength.[10] He does not expect you to fail. If you do, He still loves and forgives you. But He assumes you will succeed because He has given you all things you will ever need relative to life and godliness.[11] If there were anything else He felt you needed, or that He could have supplied you with, He would have done it. But as far as God is concerned, you have *got* to make it because you have *Him!*

I have a friend who used to live in Boston. He did not see the number of people trust in Christ that others saw in the same type of situation, but those he reached were all faithful. One day I said, "Doug, why is it that so many of my men seem to fall by the wayside, while most all of yours go on?" His reply was, "I don't *let* them fall. I expect every one to keep moving." Later, I talked with some of his men. The thought of unfaithfulness to the Lord had never crossed their minds.

God believes in you. Not just because He is good at

thinking positive thoughts (though I'm sure He is), but because you are now a part of Him, and He is part of you. If we count on this, we are free from the worry that comes from uncertainties in relationships. There are no uncertainties as far as God is concerned. God said He would never leave you nor forsake you.[12]

Love Never Fails

We see that saying on dusty plaques in parlors of old homes. But, wow, is it true! Love *never* fails. *God* never fails. He never fails to love you first. He never fails to love you unconditionally. He never fails to be patient, kind, etc. etc., etc. He is on duty in your behalf twenty-four hours a day.

You Can Love Yourself

*For the whole Law is fulfilled in one word,
in the statement, "You shall love your
neighbor as yourself."*

Galatians 5:14

7.

You Can Love Yourself

The end result of God's love flowing unconditionally from Him to us is that a love response is activated within our lives. His love becomes creative; it molds us into new persons. God's love does not *demand* a change; it *produces* one.

The passage, "We love, because He first loved us"[1] tells the whole story of the creative love cycle. But there is something in between our receiving God's love and, in turn, giving it back to Him that is tremendously important. It is this in-between step that we wish to consider here.

Way back in Sunday school almost all of us, regardless or our denominational backgrounds, learned a little adage that went something like this:

> Jesus first,
> Others second,
> Yourself third.

It was a very convenient and easy slogan because the first three letters of those phrases spelled *joy*, and the kids found it easy to remember. But the divine order of that saying should go:

> Jesus loves me first,
> I love myself because He loves me,
> Now that I love myself, I am free to love others.

(That will never sell because, first, it's too long, and secondly, it spells *jin* which says nothing. However, this "new order" is, nonetheless, true.)

Before I can address myself to the challenge of loving or accepting other people as they are, I must first take *myself* as I am. And before the latter is possible, I need to know *God* loves me as I am.

Jesus said, "Love your neighbor as yourself."[2] What He meant was, "Love your neighbor just as you love yourself," or, applied conversely, "Before you can love your neighbor, you must be able to love yourself."

We get all hot and bothered about this thing of loving ourselves. Since the psychologists came on the scene with this ego bit, most of us Christians have pulled our heads back into our shells and started hating ourselves because ego was, all of a sudden, bad. But, in conversion my ego acquires a forwarding address. I am no longer under the domain of the flesh; I am now controlled by the Holy Spirit. The real me is a new person, residing in the realm of the new life of the human spirit. I have been reborn.

Loving ourselves is crucial to loving others — even God! Paul came right out and said it in describing love on the human plane, in the context of marriage. "So husbands

ought also to love their own wives as their own bodies.
He who loves his own wife loves himself."[3] It's the age-
old principle that before I can straighten out other people's
houses, I'd better get my own in order. If it doesn't work
at home, it surely will not work with others.

What does it mean to love ourselves? Basically, it is to
see ourselves as God sees us. The trouble is that we traditionally say that God sees us as dirty, rotten sinners, and
we stop right there. God sees us as dirty, rotten, *forgiven*
sinners! He looks at us as part of His new creation, part
of the new man, vessels unto honor, uniquely His, meet for
the Master's use.[4] His word to personal sin is, "and such
were some of you."[5] He is satisfied with us because of the
presentation of us faultless before Him by His Son. In His
sight we are winners, not losers; overcomers, not overcome;
we are a kingdom of priests unto God.[6]

Loving ourselves also involves accepting our weaknesses
as well as our strengths. I, personally, stormed into the
kingdom of God with, among other things, a bad temper.
Not many of my friends know this because I have become
so experienced and professional at hiding it behind my
external behavior. Rather than try to change my inner
make-up, I have decided to accept it as it is because God
did. That is not to say my temper is right, but it is to say
that God took me that way and forgave me. Since I accept my temper problem, I am free to accept yours. That
has changed my life. If I inwardly curse myself when I
lose my cool, I will inevitably do the same thing to you
when you lose yours. But since I do not condemn myself
over my temper problem, I tend to forget about it, and
therefore, yours does not bother me either. The result is
I can accept myself as I am and others as they are. And
the beauty of it is, as I turn my attention from myself and

my problems to Jesus Christ and His sufficiency, I have fewer anger problems. My temper no longer threatens me, because it's not the issue; Jesus Christ is.

Some friends in Kansas call this "relaxing in the Spirit," and they are right. We have been liberated by the death and resurrection of Jesus Christ to take ourselves as we are and let Him cleanse us. And He is *so* much better at that sort of thing than are we.

And before I get off this matter of self-acceptance, I want to mention the physical ramifications, too. Some of us are downright ugly. We look in the mirror in the morning and whisper to God, "How come You didn't make me good-looking? I've seen a better face on a watch."

God made us as we are for a reason. He could best be glorified in us that way. Listen to what King David says in Psalm 139 as he ponders God's feelings for His created individual:

13. For thou didst form my inward parts, thou didst knit me together in my mother's womb.
14. I praise thee, for thou art fearful and wonderful. Wonderful are thy works! Thou knowest me right well;
15. my frame was not hidden from thee, when I was being made in secret, and intricately wrought in the depths of the earth.
16. Thy eyes beheld my unformed substance; in thy book were written, every one of them, the days that were formed for me, when as yet there was none of them.
17. How precious to me are thy thoughts, O God! How vast is the sum of them! (RSV)

In Ephesians, Paul says much the same thing about God's new creation, and the principle is identical. "For we are His workmanship, created in Christ Jesus for good works, which God prepared beforehand, that we should walk in them."[7] The word "workmanship" in the Greek is the word "poetry."

Has anyone ever told you that when they made you they threw away the mold? It always draws a laugh when it's said in a crowd. But poetry is not made from a mold; it's a totally creative act. There has never been another person like you and there never will be. And your soul and your spirit are unique as well. God loves you as you are.

When I was in high school, I always wanted to be physically big. I was 6'4", but weighed only 145. I was so slender that after gym class I had to run around in the shower in order to get wet! It was the style back then to wear a V-neck sweater with only a T-shirt underneath. I would turn sideways and disappear. So I wore three or four T-shirts under my sweater just to pork up enough to be seen. My weight (or my lack of it) began to affect the real me because I did not accept myself as I was. I was down on God because I was not heavier.

Because God loves me and created me as I am — body, soul, and spirit — I am able, through knowing Him, to accept and be thankful for myself the way I am. (Now I've been adding some pounds, so this illustration may soon be invalid!)

During a recent trip to Memphis, I became engaged in an in-depth conversation with a good friend who is from Atlanta. He is somewhat younger than I and is very much interested in and contemplative of the idea of marriage.

"I am ready to fall in love and settle down," he said, "but I don't really trust myself. I have this basic fear that I will meet a girl who is everything I want, fall in love, but then, at a later time, meet someone else I really feel is better. It is because of this fickleness of my own heart that marriage tends to scare me off."

The subject of marriage is one of my favorites. There has probably never been a mortal soul who is more enthusiastic over the institution of marriage than I. And I am very closed-minded on the subject. I feel that I ended up with the best, most beautiful, most lovable girl in the whole world.

"Tom," I remarked to my friend, "I can see what you mean, but that thought has never presented itself to me as a possibility. I accept Marilyn as she is, and she takes me as I am. We want only each other. She loves me with all my faults and inadequacies, and I love her with hers. And our love creates in each other a deeper and broader capacity to love. Instead of our affection waning or remaining static, it just keeps growing."

We turned to the passage in Ephesians 5 regarding loving our wives as our own bodies. "Let me ask you a question," I said. "Do you feel there are other men in the world better looking than you?"

"Of course," he replied, laughing.

I mentioned the name of a close, mutual friend who is regarded by most people as very handsome. "Is he better equipped physically than are you?"

Tom agreed right away.

"Let me ask — whose body would you rather have, yours or his?"

"I'd rather have mine," he said.

"Why?"

"I'm not sure," he said. "I just like it."

We both chortled at ourselves for talking this way. I don't think either of us had ever verbalized these thoughts before.

"Now," I continued, "say that you fall deeply in love with a wonderful girl. She is wild about you. You see her faults and don't care. You love her anyway. She is aware of your flaws, but that doesn't matter to her in the least. She loves you beyond all that. God gives you peace about the relationship and you become one — man and wife. She is now yours. She *belongs* to you. She and you have become one flesh. Her love thrills you past description. And you discover that the love you give to her delights her immensely. She tells you so.

"Now in the course of everyday life you will meet thousands of other women. But Tom, and this is basic, whose body do you want; to which person do you feel continually drawn?"

"Man, I've never thought about that before," he answered. "You really *do* love your wife like you love yourself. She is a part of you."

Love is so creative. It provides a security pocket out of which you never want to escape. The thought of closing out on Jesus Christ has never been in my mind since I became a Christian. We have a love thing going that is so much better than *anything* else. He has created within me a desire to be with Him forever. Likewise, the thought of snooping around for a new life's partner is equally irrelevant. Other women will be winning beauty contests and charm awards from now till Armageddon. That doesn't bait me a bit. I've got something going for me that's so strong, I am scarcely aware of any kind of option or alternative.

Divorce in this country is at an all-time high, according to government statistics. In many cities and counties the number of divorces are ahead of the marriages. People do not know how to love each other. Apart from a spiritual birth, God's kind of love is impossible to see and understand. The world says, "You love me first, then I'll love

you. But my love will stop if you do not do what I say."
All man has to go on are performance-centered relationships. Since people are rarely accepted on any basis other
than what they do, they have no alternative orientation
by which to accept others. The disease spreads from the
individual to our society. And the world-system is born.
In the system unconditional, undemanding love cannot work
because the entire structure of society militates against it.

Part of salvation is being saved *out* of the world. The
church is a brand-new society. It is part of God's Kingdom,
and love is what holds the Kingdom together. Marriage,
too, is a product of that Kingdom. That is why marriage
often does not and cannot work in the world. It is out of
its natural element. We have tried to transplant it from
the Kingdom back into the world, and we do not succeed.

When a husband, as an individual, and a wife, as an individual, are born of God and know Him, they *experience*
His perfect love. They know that it comes by grace, not
by merit. They believe that they are constantly abiding in
forgiveness, and their actions form no obstruction to their
oneness with God. It is here where they can then accept
themselves. They accept their flaws and their weaknesses
because God does. They do not promote them or endorse
them, but they do accept them. And they no doubt find
that as they forget their failures, as God already has, and
simply walk with Him, these liabilities will tend to disappear. And as they love and accept themselves without
condemnation, they are capable of loving and accepting
each other the same way — God's way!

Which of these two situations would keep me more faithful to my wife? If, before I embark on a short journey, she
were to say to me, "I love you, but you better not cheat
on me while you're gone." Or if she would say, "My love

for you is so deep that even if you were to turn from me, my love would not alter one bit!"

Those words need never be articulated. It's the heart attitude, the unspoken thing, that says it. But as we know and feel God's love for us, from Him through the cross of Christ, and from others through the body of Christ, a new life of love will be *created* in us. First Corinthians 13 will become our life. It will work in our own lives, in our love for God and in our love for others.

The First-Century
Love-In

*Behold, how good and how pleasant
it is for brethren to dwell together in unity!*

Psalm 133:1

8.

The First-Century Love-In

The church of the first century was a spectacle to behold. It was composed of, to say the least, Christian activists. As a result of the strength of their message it is recorded at one point, "nearly the whole city assembled to hear the word of God." [1] A group of men within the church were referred to, on another occasion, as "these men who have upset the world . . . ." [2]

What a contrast, unfortunately, to the church of today. The contemporary church, entwined in the intricacies of social issues and political views (and there is obviously nothing wrong with interests in these areas as such), has managed to help keep the Christian Gospel one of the world's best kept secrets. With little fear of contradiction, it can be said the average church member is a secret service Christian. I like the title "Lady Clairol Christians" — only the Lord knows for sure! We rarely *say* anything about our faith. Could it be that we do not *experience* a sufficient amount of the reality of the living Christ to talk about Him? Is there a chance that what we today call the body of Christ is but a caricature of the true?

The Basis of the Church

In the New Testament the basis of identity with the body of Christ was simply faith in Him — a live and vital relationship with Him. The church was held together by love. As a matter of fact there was no membership. There were no church rolls or communicant versus non-communicant members. The issue was not membership, but fellowship. The evidence indicates that these people in whom the Holy Spirit lived just gravitated together naturally. "But none of the rest dared to associate with them; however, the people held them in high esteem."[3] The type of relationship people had with each other and with God was, in and of itself, enough to draw the lines of identity. It would be fair to say that impending persecution had something to do with it. Mutual fear of a common enemy will draw any group closer together. But that was not the basis of their unity. Their forgiveness through the blood of Christ, their receptivity to His love, and their eager hope for the kingdom of God were the overwhelming cohesive factors in their togetherness. Guidelines for official membership were unknown.

But what about today's churches? Most all will agree the basis of unity is in Jesus Christ. But if this is true, what is the source of all the apparent frosting on the cake?

On one hand, in addition to a long list of doctrinal qualifications, the membership committee of one church, in so many words, may well ask, "Do you dance, drink, smoke, or chew, or run around with girls who do?"

On the other hand, several visits to a church of a more liberal persuasion will often uncover a strong current of do's and don't's in quite another direction. By the time you have digested three or four sermons, you get the feeling that if you are not against the war in Southeast Asia, an active supporter of legislation to instigate open housing in your area, and have not participated in at least one demonstration in an inner-city ghetto, you have no hope at all of welcome in the fold.

What a deprivation! Where does the Holy Spirit come into all of this? When are we going to cease preaching just the good views and start talking about the good news? This relates so closely to the matter of being *led* of God. Instead of obeying conservative convictions or liberal mandates, when will we learn to trust the indwelling Spirit of God as our basis for life?

Today, most Christians are banded together by denominations, each emphasizing its own distinction. Some Christians are non-denominational or anti-denominational, so they cling together under that banner. One man I know defines a denomination as "a group of people meeting together under a common denominator other than Jesus Christ." I cannot help but feel that what God wants to do is so big *no* group could contain it!

They were so much more free in the first century. Their love was not based upon their choice for Roman proconsul or whether or not some of their number happened to slip in to see the local chariot race on Saturday afternoon. They loved because *God loved them.*

Does this mean that morality does not count? Is this to nullify the law of God? Should purity of doctrine be ignored? With Paul I say, "May it never be!"[4] What we are talking about here is a matter of cause and effect. Paul, in the Book of Colossians, had just finished telling his friends to be carefully aware to exhibit compassion, kindness, humility, gentleness, and patience. But then he added, "And beyond all these things put on love, which is the perfect bond of unity."[5] The oneness of the Church is built upon love. It was so in the first century; it must be so today. Where unconditional love and acceptance in the Spirit are present and active, doctrinal purity, morality, and obedience are bound to result.

We say we trust the Holy Spirit. We tell men that if they respond to Jesus Christ and allow Him to invade their lives, He will launch them upon a new adventure of living. But do we believe it ourselves? If so, why then do we erect so many superficial, anthropomorphic guidelines just to "insure" that God will succeed? Is it, perhaps, we who claim to know Him who are in practice saying that He is dead? Was Paul mistaken when he wrote, "Therefore if any man be in Christ, he is a new creature; the old things passed away; behold, new things have come"?[6]

And upon what basis should we demand that all men cross their "t's" and dot their "i's" the way we do as a prerequisite for fellowship? Was it not Christ Himself who said, "Do not judge lest you be judged yourselves"?[7] If God loves me and receives me as I am, why should I not do the same for others in the household of faith? Paul wrote, "Now accept the one who is weak in faith, but not for the purpose of passing judgment on his opinions."[8] It is when men are loved and trusted in the body of Christ that they begin to be molded into the image of the Lord Jesus through the Holy Spirit.

THE CHURCH AND THE WORLD

The word "church" means, in its purest form, a group of people met for a definite reason. It is often translated, "the called out ones." The Greek word *ecclesia*, from which we derive our English word "church," first appeared in the fourth century B.C. when it was utilized to describe a Greek senate. Later, the word came to refer to any group of people meeting together for a precise purpose.

There's no inherent sense of extra-real religiosity about the word. Its basic New Testament reference is to a portion of humanity that happens to name Christ as Lord over all. They compose His body here on earth, His special, beloved society. And, on this basis, everybody counts. All are significant.

The Early Church saw their calling out of the world far more clearly than we do today. In fact, it is an intriguing phenomenon that the hippie philosophy has come much closer to a Biblical insight into the hopelessness of the world than have many of us Christians. The establishment is void, temporary, meaningless, they say. Why get ahead in the world-system when it really has nothing to offer? As one international student said, "We make it to the top of the ladder, only to find out the ladder has been leaning against the wrong wall."

It is the hippie solution which so cruelly draws men and women into the place of darkness. They have no alternative. In a sense, they themselves become a "hippie establishment."

Jesus' analysis of the problem was radical by present standards. His kingdom was not of this world. His program was to call people out of the world, not involve them in its system. He said:

". . . you are not of the world . . . ."[9]

". . . I chose you out of the world . . . ."[10]

". . . the world hates you . . . ."[11]

". . . they are not of the world, even as I am not of the world."[12]

Jesus tunes us in to the love of God, turns us on through the Spirit of God, but instead of having us drop out, it's called out — *ecclesia*, the called out ones — called out of the world system to Himself. His solution was a new society, a new order — the church, His body. We're *in* the world, but not *of* it.

(I must confess that I get a bit irritated when I hear parents send their kids off to college so they can "get ahead in the world." *Christian* parents. God's plan is for us to rule with Him in His Kingdom, not being people tied to this world.)

His Kingdom, His city, is the hope of our calling. Through Him we have dominion over the earth — that's His purpose for us *now*. And the church of the first century saw this! Nothing wrong with school, business, the professions, or the arts per se. But these are of this world, and would to God we saw them as such. Sure we need to make a living; sure we need to provide for our wives and kids. God says that.[13] But our enchantment is in the heavenlies. We can be free from the bondage of human achievement as an end in itself. We need not be dominated by our surroundings; the domination of our environs belongs to us because we are members of the body of Christ. What a thrill to live creatively, unencumbered by the world, *experiencing* our oneness and dominion in the body!

CHRISTIAN MATURITY

The early Christians, I think, saw themselves as being in Christ in a different sense from what we do. It was not so much, "*I* am growing up in Christ," as "*We* are being built up in Christ." We hear much today about a personal relationship with Christ, and there is no other way to enter His body than on a personal basis. But we don't stop there. God wants to build us up together. His plan is a building, not just a bunch of individual stones. Coming to Christ is individual; maturity in Christ is corporate.[14] We were never meant to be little islands in ourselves, struggling on our own to "get to know the Lord better." God wants us to draw together and be one.

Along these lines, something beautiful is taking place on the college campuses of this land. Students are starting to see and experience the reality of the body of Christ. On many campuses that I know about (and I'm sure many more that I don't know about), students who know Jesus Christ are spontaneously gravitating together into small cells with Christ. Often they have the Lord's Supper together; some are even baptizing their own converts. They are seeing themselves as an expression of the church. No man is organizing this thing, and nobody is promoting it; it's just happening.

Listen to the comments in this letter from a student at a Big Ten university:

> We weren't sure how to proceed because of numerous warnings about trying to have body life on human effort. But we knew for sure we wanted it; we *had* to have it. We thought the safest thing would be to just trust the Holy Spirit to lead us.
>
> At a retreat last weekend, after the Saturday night message, we got together to pray and share, and this was the high point of the whole retreat for us. It used to be almost an ordeal for us to think of enough to pray about for 10 minutes, but for 2½ hours we prayed, shared, and sang. It was such a new experience it about blew our minds. We

were in the Spirit like none of us had ever before experienced.

We planned to meet again Sunday night and I expected 5 or 6, but the house was packed and it was like Saturday night all over again. It's hard to get used to being led by the Spirit and not by human leaders. At first when someone wanted to pray or sing a song, they would ask for permission, but gradually it began to be more like the New Testament church life: one of us suggested a song to sing, another shared something from the Word, another told what God had been teaching him. Everyone fit in and we all benefited.[15]

I've never felt such love and oneness and joy in a group situation before. You could almost cut it. Time passed by before we knew it, and we can't wait until the next time. We're meeting Sunday nights for sure and maybe Wednesdays.

What is phenomenal is that the Spirit has shown all of the kids this stuff at about the same time. Kids who never liked to witness share that they *want* to for the first time. And now we have something real to bring new Christians to that isn't a fake or show.

The students see the body of Christ as it is much faster than we who have been Christians "too long." They have less to unlearn than we do! Perhaps God will use the Christians of the coming generation as His means for bringing an awakening to the entire body.

FUNCTIONS OF THE BODY

It is a compelling fact that, in the writings of Matthew, Jesus says of His church, " . . . and the gates of hell shall not prevail against it."[16] But why, then, as we look at the structure of the church in our period in history, *are* the gates of hell prevailing against it? It is fighting for members. It is sponsoring contests to lure new people into its halls. It is such that people do not really seem to care if they attend. When asked why they come, many say it is their responsibility as Christians to do so. In the first century it was *not* their responsibility; it was their privilege. They really *wanted* to be together.

The love of God also motivated people in the Early Church in the area of social concerns. But let me say at this point that their thinking with regard to their function was not categorized in areas of church duty as ours is today — such as discipline, social outreach, evangelism, etc. They just helped people. It was not program-oriented; it was people-oriented. People within the body of Christ, living in the reality of their oneness in Him, offered themselves as helpers in times of need, just as in our physical bodies, our cells tend to build each other up if a breakdown occurs. Both on the day of Pentecost and in the crisis of the widows and orphans in Acts 6, the power of person-to-person love in action in the young church is seen in a magnificent way.

And what about this matter of evangelism? There are three distinct types of evangelism recorded in the Bible. One is mass evangelism, and the events on the day of Pentecost are those most usually cited in this regard. Secondly, we see the type often represented by Philip and the Ethiopian Eunuch, or Jesus and the woman at the well — personal evangelism. But there is a third means of evangelism that is predominant in the Acts and the epistles[17] — body evangelism. It is where the body of Christ is moving under the direction of the Holy Spirit and new life inevitably results. It is the "and the Lord was adding to their number day by day those who were being saved"[17] type of outreach.

On the physical plane, a healthy body has no difficulty in reproducing after its kind. It would be silly to tell a young married couple, "Look, if you are going to adequately fulfill your awesome tasks as a couple bound together in matrimonial oneness, then you had better start having some kids — if for no other reason than to prove that you are married!" That just is not the way it works. Children are the normal result of a human partnership. In fact, the presence of children is so absolutely normal that today we are spending millions of dollars per annum, not to aid human reproduction, but to abate it! What a thrilling day for the church of God if, for some reason, spiritual procreation got out of hand. Perhaps that explains why the presence of a spiritual awakening is viewed by most of us as extra-normal. As one minister put it, "We are so spiritually cold that when someone comes along with a 98.6, everybody thinks he has a fever."

The Early Church was bound together by the love of God. They knew He accepted them, and they enjoyed an attitude of acceptance toward each other. What they experienced when they were together had a drawing power on those without. God was so real in their midst, that becoming a part of their fellowship was tantamount to receiving Jesus Christ, and receiving Jesus Christ meant, by the same token, a new identity with God's people. It went without saying that all who loved and trusted Him were considered to be a part. Not to be a part of the first-century church was not to be a part of Jesus Christ at all.

It is interesting to note that the case of church discipline in First Corinthians 5 is germane to this whole concept of identity with the body of Christ.[18] Here was a man committing incest. After repeated counsel, he was turned over to Satan. *But look how this was done.* Paul did not get on long distance, ring up Area Code 666, dial the number, and say, "I'm sending another one down." He simply separated the offender from a visible identity and fellowship with the body. Jesus was so much a true and real part of that community of believers, that to be apart from them was to be apart from the Lord and in the hands of the devil himself.[19] And yet twenty centuries later, and I believe I'm speaking of the great majority of people, we can join or leave a given assembly of the church and it means little or nothing either way. Or if we are asked to leave one church, we can go down the street and join another. The movement has reverted to a monument.

In Hebrews 12 we read, "Whom the Lord loves He disciplines, and He scourges every son whom he receives."[20] The cause of God's discipline is always found in His love. Also, later on in that same chapter it is recorded that God does not discipline those who do not belong to Him. Just as we do not spank the neighbor's kids, so God does not get after those who are not entrusting themselves to His care.

The guilty party of First Corinthians 5, by the way, was back on the track by the time Paul addressed his second letter to the church in that city.[21] And it is doubtful that a series of mimeographed postcards sent out each month inviting him to a potluck family night had much to do with it. He simply missed their love. He felt part of his very life had been taken away, and he wanted "in" again. Had they gossiped his sin about town, he would have been forever lost to their fellowship. Though it was sin that had driven him from them, it must have been love that drew him back.

CHURCH STRUCTURE

When the church was launched, it met in homes. There were no "church" buildings until the third century.[22] Elaborate physical structures were erected under a new church and state plan inaugurated during the reign of Constantine.[23] The seeds of institutionalism began to take root.

Is the presence or lack of an ecclesiastical edifice a crucial issue? It really depends upon how God leads the people. But let's be honest. Was it He who superintended the initial building program 1700 years back? With the tradition once established, was it He who led it to continue? What would be His purpose in taking something that had shaken the world in the first hundred years and progressively removing from it the freedom and spontaneity upon which it thrived?

In practical terms, there is no comparison between the infant church and the structure of today, as far as simplicity and effectiveness are concerned. There was no building program, and thus no excessive budget drain. Arguments over seating arrangements and carpet hues at the meeting of the building committee were non-existent. And if some wrong doctrine crept into the group and it began going sour, they were free to leave and move on to another living room. Today it is more complex. There is a building to maintain, a janitor to pay, a mortgage to retire, a minister to support, plus the commitment to the contractor to begin work on an addition of an east wing next April. Even if the reason to exist departs, there is little alternative but to keep going. And what remains is a mere shell of what before held life. Now, instead of the life of the body determining its structure, its structure determines the life. Thus, the establishment is born.

Many churches are facing this problem by attempting to establish small groups within the church to provide a base of identity for what may be hundreds, or even thousands, of members. These groups often meet in homes.[24] Some of these succeed; some of them fail. Much of the problem is in the people not knowing exactly of what they are a part. Theologically, these small groups are really churches in themselves, but for some reason we are hesitant to refer to them as such.

A stirringly significant by-product of the love in the hearts of the early Christians was the unity in the Spirit which they possessed. There were no hierarchies. Everyone was on the same level. They even called Paul by his first name. (By the way, what *was* his last name?) Certainly there were those within the fellowship who were recognized by the people as the spiritual leaders — the elders, deacons, overseers. But these men felt no need to flex their organizational muscles. There were none to flex. Even in the case of Onesimus, Philemon's runaway slave, Paul wrote to the latter to express confidence in his walk with the Lord. There was no pulling of rank. Paul's attitude was, "I do not order you to receive him, I just appeal to you as a brother in Christ."[25] There were no big shots. All were equal as brothers in the body of Christ. What a challenge for our thinking. Are we going to unite in the power of the Spirit or through an organizational chart?

THE REFORMATION

In the 16th century a young, somewhat hotheaded German monk rediscovered a fundamental truth that had been lost to the Christian faith for hundreds of years: salvation by grace through faith. Once again life began to reappear and the body began to regroup. What he said was of God. He was mightily used and blessed. We know the man as Martin Luther; the movement was the Reformation. But soon, speaking in a broad historical perspective, the movement died and institutionalism again extinguished the flame of the Spirit. Small prairie fires subsequently sprang up, but gradually burned down to a smoldering norm. Wesley emerged two centuries after Luther, and through Luther's writings on Romans he realized for his era of history what Luther had found two hundred years before. Perhaps the greatest renewal since Pentecost occurred at that time; yet today the visible results of that surge are but structural remains. The life has, for the most part, withered.

There was another group present at the time of Luther who have gone down in church history as the theological "bad guys." They were known as the Anabaptists. They were doctrinally with Luther on faith and grace. They liked what they heard. But they went one step further. With perception ahead of their time, they foresaw that what Luther was saying would not take hold with any permanence unless there was another element. What these Reformers had, they said, was fine. But they needed new containers, new wineskins, in which to put the discovery. The doctrine of salvation by grace through faith is well and good. But the contents of the truth of the Holy Spirit will not last unless they are placed in the environment of the freedom of the Holy Spirit.

They called for restitution. The solution, they said, was to bring the church itself back up to the point where it was when the truth of grace was first made known. Their voices went unheard. The Reformation was born and died. But they were right. And today, we need call again for restitution.

What Lies Ahead?

The move, at this present hour, is to *structural* unity. Let's bring everybody together under one roof, comes the naive call. We'll organize it, delegate it, supervise it, and we'll live happily ever after. If what we have today on the local level leaves us wanting, think of the outcome of this

abortive attempt by self-appointed ecclesiastical superbun-
nies to compound for us all what already has failed to work!

Some see today's church as irrelevant; others see the
"New Testament church" as it truly should be; many see
both. But as it has been in every age of awakening and
renewal from Pentecost on, God, not men, must through
His Spirit provide the leadership for change. Jesus said,
"*I* will build *My* church."[26] (Italics mine.) That a change
needs to come is clear. To simply be against the structure
as a means of change does little. Let us rather ask God
to lead us together into the true life of the body of Christ.
And if what has been said in this chapter does no more
than "sow seed" to that end, its mission will be complete.
Certainly this writer is in no position, and never shall be
in a position, either to define or direct the means of change.

The love and trust which come from God are expressed
within that body, the church. That is the way He planned
it. No one has ever improved upon His plan. When He
directed it, it flourished; when men took over, it failed. At
this point in history, when God's voice in the world seems
pallid and weak, dare we stand and call again, two thousand years later, for the emergence of the true and living
church?

The Road to Freedom

And an highway shall be there, and a way,
and it shall be called The way of holiness;
the unclean shall not pass over it; but it
shall be for those: the wayfaring men,
though fools, shall not err therein.

Isaiah 35:8

If therefore the Son shall make you free,
you shall be free indeed.

John 8:36

9.

The Road to Freedom

God's love not only makes possible the complete cleansing of our lives allowing us a fresh, new confidence before Him, but He also declares us free and unshackled from the law. Through Christ we have been removed from the monotonous, tiring trails of performance and religious effort and placed upon what Isaiah the prophet called the "highway of holiness." It is a spacious, scenic, and, unfortunately, seldom-traveled road to freedom.

Aside from the engulfing de-emphasis today upon the body of Christ and His work on the cross in our behalf, if I had to name what I feel to be the next greatest plague upon Christendom at this moment in history, it would be our corporate ignorance that we as believers have been declared free men. And not only have we who call ourselves Christians become entwined with behavior-centered as opposed to belief-centered relationships to Christ, but those who exist without the gates of God's earthly reign are kept from Him by our oft-told insistence upon "Christian conformity." We say we are building moral fences within which they can move. But in reality we are saying, "We cannot trust the Holy Spirit to make you holy, so we will."

A small group of us were addressing the members of a prominent social fraternity at UCLA. After the meeting, among several men who expressed their interest in knowing Jesus Christ was one young man who insisted he meet with someone in our group who would be available just as soon as possible.

Over coffee the following morning, he said, "I would give my eyeteeth to have what you men have. But there's one thing holding me back."

"What's that?" my friend replied.

"Witnessing," he said.

"What do you mean?" we asked.

"I know good and well that if I give my heart to Christ, I'll have to start telling everyone I know how to get saved," he muttered.

"Where did you get that idea?"

"It's no idea. Some people I know who are Christians told me so. They said if you trust Christ, that's part of your responsibility, along with praying, reading the Bible, going to . . . ."

"Just a minute," my friend interrupted. "God says He takes us as we are. It's strictly a matter of trusting Him. There are no price tags attached."

"Aw, come on," he objected. "You guys are out witnessing. What do you mean, you don't have to?"

"We're doing it because we *want* to. It's a tremendous thing to share the life of Christ with people, but that doesn't have a thing to do with becoming a Christian."

We went on to explain to him the greatness of God's love, and how at the cross, Jesus Christ so totally removed the barriers from him to God, that even if there were something he wanted to do to help deserve it, he couldn't.

"Are you telling me that I could accept Jesus Christ right now, and never do a thing in return, and He'd still accept me?" he inquired, almost puzzled.

We assured him that was so.

"Well, if you *promise* me that Christ will come into my life today, and that I'll never have to witness, I'll accept Him."

"We promise," came our reply.

We prayed together, and he invited Jesus Christ to become his Lord and Saviour. We went on to explain to him that God had forgiven all sin — past, present, and future — everything he ever had or ever would do was placed upon Jesus Christ. We told him about his new life that would never end.

"This is the most fantastic thing I have ever heard," he responded. "I can't believe that I didn't have to do anything to get it."

He walked back over to the fraternity house. It was about 10:00 in the morning. He approached the first friend he saw and said, "I've got to tell you the most amazing thing I have ever heard. Today I realized that I could invite Jesus Christ to come into my life, and that I wouldn't have to witness or do anything, and He'd still come in. This is the greatest thing I have ever heard. Isn't that fantastic!" And by evening, he had spread the word around the entire fraternity. Because he didn't *have* to.

When are we going to learn that righteousness comes not by works but by faith?

I visit different churches in my travels Sunday after Sunday, and nine times out of ten the message is: "We must pray more; how many hours of devotions have you had this week? Will you say a word for Christ at the office this week? Are you obeying Him as you ought?" And what we really need is *life*. But instead death prevails, and the people leave, friendly, saying good-by, shaking hands, but immaculately unchanged.

Paul writes to this whole issue of law and grace throughout his epistles. In Romans 7 his descriptions and applications of the futility of law-living are so graphic. He teaches, "For while we were in the flesh, the sinful passions, which were aroused by the Law, were at work in the members of our body to bear fruit for death" (Romans 7:5).

In this passage, two elements are necessary for sin to be produced: *sinful passions* and *the law*. The sinful passions are the seat of rebellion within us, the thing about us that deep-down enjoys doing it wrong. The law, on the other hand, serves as the object against which the sinful passions rebel. And, of course, it is not simply against the law of God that we rebel; it is against law as a principle* as well.

---

* We often fail to see the identity between "law as a principle" and the Old Testament law. Law is generally understood as the written Old Testament law, and that law, it is understood, has been fulfilled in Christ. However, Christians find themselves bothered by law as a principle, out of which often emerges "Christian law." The misunderstanding may be quickly dispelled when it is seen that the *truth* of the Ten Commandments existed long before they were given to Moses. "Thou shalt not kill" was valid way back when Cain murdered Abel. Man understood law as a principle when he ate of the fruit of the tree of knowledge of good and evil. However, because of sin, he rationalized evil to be good and good to be evil. So God made the law absolute on Mt. Sinai that man would know the true *content* of law as a principle. In their effect upon people, both types of law have the same result. The truth of God is eternal. His principles of law were simply made clear in the giving of the Old Testament law.

Be it the law of God or the principle of law, man, because of his passion for sin, sets out to disobey. Paul himself says, "I would not have come to know sin except through the Law; for I would not have known about coveting if the Law had not said, 'You shall not covet'" (Romans 7:7). The law energizes our capacity to sin; it turns our sin passions on, live and in color. And the Apostle states the way he came to know sin, in this case coveting or lusting, was that the law said, "Don't do it."

Paul goes on to say, "But sin, taking opportunity through the commandment, produced in me coveting of every kind; for apart from the Law sin is dead" (Romans 7:8). What a statement! Why is it that sin is produced in us? Just as when I, as an earthly father, say "No-no" to my child, and he goes ahead and does it anyway, so God says "no" to us and He gets a similar response. The problem is not that we are wrong in issuing the orders. The breakdown occurs within our hearts; the sin passions rebel and do it anyhow!

What is the solution? To let my child become lawless? Not at all. And that is not God's answer to the dilemma either. He has another plan. The Ford Motor Company announced one year, "Now, there's a better idea from Ford." God also made a similar announcement one year: "When He said, 'A new covenant,' He has made the first obsolete."[1] Now, there's a better idea from God!

"I will put My Laws into their minds, and I will write them upon their hearts."[2] God's new plan, instead of the impersonal, demanding law from without, is the personal and loving Holy Spirit from within.

Among the reasons that God revealed His law in the first place are three: (1) He wanted to demonstrate to us what true holiness produces, and that He *is* holiness; (2) He, by allowing us to see the written manifestation of holiness, permitted us to look into the legal mirror and find our sinful reflection, that we do not nor cannot measure up; and (3) to make us sin more.

Look at Romans 5:20: "And the Law came in that the transgression might increase; but where sin increased, grace abounded all the more." Part of the reason God put His people under law was that sin might increase. Paul wrote in another place, "The power of sin is the law."[3] Why in the world would God give something to the human race that would eventuate in further sin? Because through our misery and frustration of first, *wanting* to do better (we found out the difference between good and evil from the tree of the knowledge of good and evil in Genesis 3), and second, trying our best to be good and never meeting the expectations of either ourselves or God, we would call out to God in repentance and trust in His fulfillment of the law, Jesus Christ. In that sense, the law becomes our schoolmaster or personal tutor[4] which leads us to Christ.

God is fussy about this business of holiness. His standards are pure and absolute; there are no half-tones of gray. Trying to be holy, therefore, becomes doubly grave in its outcome. Even if we were to improve in our performance according to either man's or God's standards, it would never be good enough. So why waste our time and suffer the fatigue of failure in the arena of self-effort? Part of the purpose in Jesus' death and resurrection was to break us out of the penitentiary of human works and allow us to rest in His righteousness. If we insist on trying to obey the rules, we will sin all the more.

A man decides he is controlled by thoughts of lust and sets out to lick the problem. He gets up in the morning, and his first thoughts are, "Today, I will not lust. Today, I will not lust." He may even ask God's assistance. By midmorning, he is so captured by his intentions against lusting, that all he thinks about is lust. He becomes caught in his own trap.

A family builds a beautiful new home just across the street, the entire front of which is plate glass. Other than admiring the home, nobody thinks much more about it. Then one day a man on the other side of town builds a home exactly like it, with the front constructed of plate glass. But he puts a sign out on his front lawn which warns, "Please do not throw stones through this window." Which one will be broken first?

The law just doesn't work as a *modus operandi* of living. The Holy Spirit does. God never intended His commandments to produce holiness. He gave them to show us what holiness is and how impossible it is to achieve it. As a matter of fact, adherence to the law simply produces more sin.

Listen to what Paul declares in Romans 7:6: "But now we have been released from the Law, having died to that by which we were bound, so that we serve in newness of the Spirit and not in oldness of the letter." We are free people! Free to do that which we truly desire *because* we have been made a new creation.

At this point some may object. Certainly we are free from the law, but we are not free to do that which we please. I would never trust my desires.

But wait a minute. Was it not God who said, "Delight thyself also in the Lord; and he shall give thee the desires of thine heart"?[5]

Let's take it back a step or two. In all my interaction with people, and I am talking now about those who do not claim to know Christ, I have never met a person whose true desire is to be evil. I speak constantly in college fraternities, to athletic teams, to business and social clubs, and I meet people who genuinely want to be changed. I am not saying that they are *not* morally decadent; many are. But they are looking for a way out! Individuals, for the most part, I believe, are not looking for ways to sin more and to get further into depression and guilt. They are searching for a means of escape.

It is this "way out" that Jesus came to give. And the basic change He makes for most of us is not so much a new hunger for a better life, but rather a new possibility and power for a whole new life. Man has known the difference between good and evil all along, according to Romans 3. His lack has been the means of attainment.

So when Jesus Christ invades our hearts and lives He comes to fulfill our desires, to give us the "desires of our hearts."

Let me ask, isn't your true desire to be a man or woman of God? Mine certainly is. That is not to say that my behavior is commensurate with that desire 100% of the time. But my true desire is to be righteous.

If you are a Christian, and, being honest with yourself, you know you have a desire to break away and raise hell, your problem is most likely that you have been living under the law for so long that you've forgotten what the Holy Spirit is really like.

It is here where we desperately need each other. To be free in Christ on a personal basis is mandatory, but there is still more. I need the fellowship of other free men, that I might experience with them their freedom, and they, mine. The check and balance for a child of God is not rules, but relationships — with Him and with each other. We need one another experientially as brothers and sisters in Christ far more than we know, and not just in business and organizational structures either. We need to function together mutually as members of the visible body of Christ.

Jesus makes us alive — alive to ourselves, to our real desires, to others, and to Him. He wasn't kidding about abundant life.[6] His great desire is that we might live life at its best: that our wills might be restored to oneness with Him.

I remember just after my own conversion how eager I was to know Christ better, in a deeper, intimate way. Many of the people who told me about the joys of being a Christian, I observed, fellowshiped with Him in the Scriptures. So I deduced that I could learn of Him in this way, too.

I had a job that summer working nights in a commercial bakery. It would be 3:00 or so in the morning before I would get home. My usual practice was to hop in bed with my Bible and read it, often until the birds were singing or until it was light outside. Nobody ever told me to do this; I just did.

My growth spiritually was tremendous. God spoke to me with clarity and power during those early morning hours, and He used those times to give a foundation to my Christian life that was without parallel.

Later that summer I was invited to attend a two-week Christian conference. God taught me many valuable lessons during that time. One evening, however, a sincere, well-meaning speaker made this statement: "If you want to be a man of God, you must spend no less than one hour per day reading His Word."

I am a sensitive person at heart. And for sure, I wanted to be a man of God. So from that time on, for the next several months, I laboriously read the Bible. School began a week after the conference, the start of my senior year. I made a grim attempt to stick with it an hour a day. Previously, I had read many times for two, three, sometimes even four hours a day; now one hour was next to impossible. I would remove my wrist watch, lay it down on my desk, and time myself. Even if I completed the hour, I was learning virtually nothing. It had all become duty.

Then one day, someone dropped the line, "No Bible, no breakfast." "Alas," I thought, "here is my answer. If I just give God the opening hour of my day, my problems will be solved." But I am one of those people who don't wake up until two hours after they get out of bed. I got less out of the morning devotions than I did when I was gutting out an hour in the afternoon.

Next, I signed up for the "Read It Thru in '62" campaign in my church. It took me fifteen months, but I read it through — Genesis all the way to Revelation! But my spirit did not expand one inch. I can recall nothing that God might have even half taught me during that ordeal.

The final gimmick was trying to listen to the Bible on record, and I invariably fell asleep. My problem all along was that I had begun to view devotions as an "act" of being spiritual. And I was trapped.

Two years ago, through understanding I was free from the law, my hunger for the Scriptures came back to life. I have never said this publicly, and I doubt I ever will, because in a book you can explain so much more than in a brief talk. But for three months I scarcely opened the Bible at all. Did God still bless? Yes. As strong as ever. Did the people I shared the Gospel with respond during that period? Sure did! How about answered prayer? All kinds of it, in fact maybe more than at any other time in my life. How could God possibly allow a thing like . . . . It's called grace. I became so sick and tired of blasting through the Bible barrier, that I quit reading it altogether.

I had a "reentry problem" from law back to grace. I did not desire to read it, so I didn't. And life was beautifully abundant and free.

After three months — and this length of time was strictly uncalculated — my hunger for the Scriptures became so strong, I could not resist reading them. Talk about happy— I was elated! It was the same joy I had had during my first weeks as a believer. Not because I stopped and then started again — and I don't recommend that route for *anyone* else — it was because the Lord gave me the desires of my heart.

If you read the Bible faithfully each morning as a free man, I *urge* and *pray* that you continue. I do not share what I have to annoy you, but to perhaps help some frustrated believers who are not like you, out from under their imitation holiness. If you have a systematic method of studying the Scriptures, and God is teaching you and blessing you in your freedom, I admire your priceless gift of discipline. *Please* keep on studying. I do not have such a gift. But let's make a bargain. I won't ask people to do it my way, if you won't insist they do it yours. (Now that bargain won't work because it's based on law. Nevertheless, I trust we know each other's hearts.)

I want to stand on the housetops of orthodox Christendom and announce to men our freedom in the Lord Jesus. Sometimes I feel like throwing a celebration, just to get together and thank Him for it. It cost Him His life, but He has set us free! He bled and died that it might be ours. We are free to be holy, free to *live*.

Occasionally, I hear a statement something like this: "We are aware that we are free from the Old Testament law, but all of us know that we are responsible to obey the law of Christ." I have no contempt for those who say this, but

I do feel it's putting the effect ahead of the cause. Obedience results from our relationship with Christ, as we have already noted, and is not the cause of it. If we truly are free, then ultimate righteousness will result. I believe we need to be patient and not instantly demand it from one another.

Another curious observation is this: If we were morally unable to keep and obey the law of Moses, how on earth will we ever obey the law of Christ which is tougher? Moses said don't kill; Jesus said if we hate someone, we have killed him. Moses said do not commit adultery; Jesus said to not even give her the eye. If all of us were running around conscientiously determining to obey the law of Christ, we'd have folks with empty eye sockets, chopped-off hands, and the church would look like a huge amputation ward.

> Oh, God, please give us eyes to see that we can't please You, even as Your children, through works of righteousness that we do. Give us divine wisdom to believe You when You say that You will reproduce Your life within us as we simply depend upon Your Spirit to do so. Show us the meaning of Your statements: "You shall know the truth, and the truth shall make you free,"[7] and "where the Spirit of the Lord is, there is liberty."[8] I pray, Father, as I write this that You will keep the devil from trying to convince fellow Christians who know they are bound up in the law to reject this truth as a brand of license and write it off as the meanderings of a young turk, and thus return again to their molds of slavery to habit and routine defeat. May we see Jesus as He really is, free at the right hand of God, and ourselves as there with Him, members of His body.

How to Succeed
in Christianity
Without Really Trying

Faithful is He who calls you, and He also will bring it to pass.

I Thessalonians 5:24

10.

How to Succeed in Christianity Without Really Trying

During the 1968 Democratic Convention in Chicago I joined a group of some thirty college students from the Chicago area to spend an evening in Lincoln Park talking with the visiting "yippies" about Jesus Christ. It was the Tuesday evening of the convention, a typically warm and balmly August night in the Windy City, and an estimated 2,000 protestors had occupied the central portion of the park. Some were intently involved in the political discussion of the crowd; the rest milled around on the perimeter of the throng, inspecting the numerous bonfires and talking with each other.

Our group had met earlier on the other side of Lake Shore Drive to pray and interact on just how to begin sharing Christ with these people across the way. As we arrived in Lincoln Park, I was somewhat confused as to what to do. I remember asking the Lord to somehow open things up for us to begin a conversation with one of the participants in the demonstration. A good friend, Don Berge, and I were together in a "two by two" arrangement.

We had been walking around the park for five minutes or so, when a young black student approached us. He seemed to be under the influence of some sort of stimulant, and I thought I smelled liquor on his breath. Standing right in front of me, he smiled and asked, "Anybody here got a high?"

"We've got a high that won't quit!" I responded.

"What's that?"

"The Holy Spirit," I said, very unsure of what his reaction would be.

"You guys got the Holy Spirit?" he asked, with apparent sincerity.

"Sure do. How about you?"

"Naw, I don't," he replied.

"Would you like to?"

"Yeah, I really would," he answered, far more serious and coherent.

Don and I began to relate to him how great it is to experience God's love and to personally count on His Son. He was interested in everything we said, and I was confident that he wanted to know Christ. Just as we were explaining what receiving Jesus Christ is all about a friend of his interrupted and quipped, "Brother, what you got?"

"Stay and listen," he said. "These guys are talking about something we really need."

We backtracked in our conversation to include the new ear, and before much time had passed both these young men were our brothers in Christ. The one we met first said later, "You don't know how glad I am you guys came by. These cats over here," he voiced with concern as he motioned to the crowd some fifty yards away, "don't have a thing."

The Holy Spirit really *is* a high that doesn't quit. He is more than just intermittent; He is new-life experience. No fix, no price, no withdrawal; just real, permanent, righteous life!

There is a great resurgence of interest today in the person and work of the Holy Spirit. People are becoming more and more aware of their personal needs and are seeking an addendum to just a "sweet by and by" message. Along with this, we are seeing that the "trying to be holy" route is a dead-end street. We do not obtain a relationship with the Holy Spirit by trying harder. He does not come to us through courageous self-effort or sincere religious achievement. He is ours by *faith*. God said so. "This is the only thing I want to find out from you. Did you receive the Spirit by the works of the law, or by hearing with faith?"[1] It is through God the Holy Spirit that we learn to succeed in Christianity without really trying. The issue is not trying but trusting.

We have talked all about the limitless and people-centered love that God is. He loves us not through our merits, but through His. Because God loves us, He forgives us and makes us free.

But there is another step to His remaking us. He fills us. He literally comes to live within our human spirits with His Holy Spirit, and it is through the Spirit of God that we become one both with Him and one with our brothers and sisters in the body of Christ. And though I believe these two onenesses are equally important — you can't have one without the other — it is upon the former that I choose to dwell.

In Romans 8, which is generally regarded as the key passage in the Scriptures on the Holy Spirit, Paul begins in verse one with a word of review just in case we failed to catch his point up until then in his book: "There is therefore now no condemnation for those who are in Christ Jesus." God condemned His Son in our place on the cross, then raised Him from death, and elevated Him to the number one spot in all creation, at His right hand. And God sees us — all who trust in Him — as being *in* Christ. In other words, God views us just as He sees His Son. As a matter of fact, I wonder if He sees any difference? You don't look at a person's head and see it differently than you see the rest of his body. He appears to you as a unit. And if *anybody, anywhere,* sees the body of Christ clearly, it certainly must be God!

Jesus will never again be under God's condemnation; He abides in His glory. What is true of Jesus Christ is true of us as His fellow heirs. We are *in* Christ. We are risen with Him to a new kind of life. And thus, we are not under the condemnation of God, nor will we ever be again! We are free from His wrath to rest in His love. He likes our program because we *are* His program. He's in this business of being God for our benefit, not just for His. From ages past, He has yearned for the day when He could be to us a God, and we could be to Him a people.[2] We're His kind of folks now. We're what He's all about, the object of His affection, the center of His attention. His day has come, through the Lord Jesus, and we are it!

Now, if God, because I am in Christ, no longer condemns me, the question I need to ask is, "Why do I so often condemn *myself?*" Can't I learn to accept me as God does? Of course. Why should we be hung up on ourselves, when God isn't? If God doesn't condemn me, there is no reason why I should condemn myself. Am I better than He is?

It all goes back to this thing on the law. If I am living under the law, be it God's laws or man's, I will constantly be engrossed in self-evaluation. But He has freed us from all that. Christ is the fulfillment of the law. And God tells us we are not condemned so He can get us out from under the stale dust of human achievement to simply count on Him to build His life within us.

"There is therefore now *no* condemnation . . . ." *God* doesn't condemn me, and *I* don't need to condemn me, either. And you can go a couple more steps. If I see myself as out from under the condemnation of God and of myself, I am free to no longer condemn others. This is the "how to" of what Jesus meant when He said, "Love your enemies,"[3] and "Forgive men for their transgressions."[4] If we see sin as dealt with in Christ, we have an outlook of forgiveness rather than an outlook of judgment toward each other.

Then, the last step in this progression is that we don't have to condemn God for what *He* does. This may sound silly, but sometimes I get short with Him. I'm angered by what He does to me. I got after Him one night when He sent some folks over who needed to know Christ. I wanted to be alone with my family. I didn't like it. Naturally, as I look back, I wouldn't have had it any other way. He knew what He did was best not only for those people, but it was best for *me*. I needed that experience. And I love Him for it. That's why James says, "Consider it all joy, my brethren, when you encounter various trials; knowing that the testing of your faith produces endurance. And let endurance have its perfect result, that you may be perfect and complete, lacking in nothing."[5]

Life in the Holy Spirit keeps us from whatever we were before we knew God. We are released not only from the spiritual and mental results of transgressions of the past, but we are free from the law of sin itself; we never *have* to sin again.

How often we are programmed to believe that sin is inevitable. "You are *going* to make mistakes again — you can't help it — you're only human. Don't expect to be perfect," we are told, "you're bound to sin again each day."

God's Word is, "For the law of the Spirit of life in Christ Jesus has set you free from the law of sin and of death" (Romans 8:2). Sin is no longer inevitable for the Christian. I never plan on sinning again — I just don't expect to. That doesn't necessarily mean I won't sin. It means that I do not plan on it. I believe I'm a new person in Christ. I am free in Him from the undertow of sin and death. God describes me that way. He tells us, "My little children, I am writing these things to you that you may *not* sin. And *if* anyone sins, we have an Advocate with the Father, Jesus Christ the righteous"[6] (italics mine).

Part of the reason, I believe, that Christians have an ongoing experience with sin is that in their hearts they truly believe they *will* do it again. Now that was true before we were freed from the law. "For what the law could not do, weak as it was through the flesh, God did: sending His own Son in the likeness of sinful flesh and as an offering for sin, He condemned sin in the flesh" (Romans 8:3). In the Holy Spirit we have been given a new life. We don't have to be controlled by sin any longer. We don't have to put up with it! And in my own experience, I find that since I have understood that I never *have* to sin again, I sin far less. It's just not the issue any longer. My consciousness, frankly, is not on sin. My identity is in Jesus Christ. The *real me* is now in Him.

If a person is not looking for anything, the odds are strong that he won't find it. In looking for righteousness to spring up in us because we have the Holy Spirit within us, sin fades far into the background. In fact, the last half of the sentence just quoted from Romans 8:3 reads, ". . . in order that the requirement of the law might be fulfilled in us, who do not walk according to the flesh, but according to the Spirit." The flip side of sin no longer being inevitable is that true righteousness in our lives and experience is *unavoidable* — if, as it says, we walk "according to the Spirit." His purpose, in this case, is to fulfill righteousness in us.

This is important: God does *not* fill us with the Holy Spirit to help us keep the law. Consciously or unconsciously, this is often what we come away with. "If I can just walk in the Spirit," we say to ourselves, "He will help me live a better life." No, it's better than that. God says the Holy Spirit already has fulfilled the law within us. Instead of telling us that He will fill us so we can keep His commandments, God tells us that because we have the Holy Spirit within, He has already graded us A+ on law-keeping! It has been fulfilled in us. Therefore, instead of plugging away to please Him, because of Jesus Christ He is already pleased. The pressure is off me to *do* anything. God says that as we just *trust* Him, the new life is produced by Him, moment by moment, within us.

Frequently the question comes, "When does the Holy Spirit come to live in me?" or "How can I be filled with the Spirit?" Read Romans 8:5-9:

5. For those who are according to the flesh set their minds on the things of the flesh, but those who are according to the Spirit, the things of the Spirit.
6. For the mind set on the flesh is death, but the mind set on the Spirit is life and peace;
7. because the mind set on the flesh is hostile toward God; for it does not subject itself to the Law of God, for it is not even able to do so;
8. and those who are in the flesh cannot please God.
9. However you are not in the flesh but in the Spirit, if indeed the Spirit of God dwells in you. But if anyone does not have the Spirit of Christ, he does not belong to Him.

Again, as in First John 1, two kinds of people are being described. There are those who are living in the flesh and those who are living by the Spirit. Look again at verse 9. What are the two classifications of people being described here? If we understand that Paul is talking about those who belong to Him as compared with those who don't — that is Christians and non-Christians — then the whole thing begins to fall into place.

I meet people who are *trying* to get the Holy Spirit and the benefits of His life. They wait around for an "experience." I have no bone to pick with those who have had an experience. But the point is, He is ours by present possession when we receive Jesus Christ. In fact it is He who is the glue which makes us one with Christ. Would it make sense that God would send Him into our lives just part way, to be the agent of our new birth, to seal us, to provide for us the down payment on eternal living, and not to complete the job of daily provision for right-now holiness? God doesn't dole out the precious Holy Spirit in bits and pieces; He is not meted and measured out to us.[7] Either we have Him or we do not. If you know Jesus as your own, thank

Him — in fact, why not take a moment and thank Him now — that the Holy Spirit is *already* yours and is *already* living within you. As has been said, "Faith is when you stop saying please and start saying thank you." Often we do not realize what God has given us until we take a moment and thank Him.

Not long ago I was reading the evening paper and I noticed a story that had come over one of the wire services, which I believe originated in Boston. The bodies of two elderly spinsters had been discovered in their modest apartment. They had died a few days earlier. An autopsy revealed they had succumbed to malnutrition. The account went on to relate that later a search had been conducted in the apartment, and hidden in the mattresses and sewn up in pillows and draperies was nearly $200,000 in cash. Here were two people who possessed abundance materially, yet they died in self-afflicted starvation.

We, as children of God, have been given the Holy Spirit. He is already ours. There is no reason at all for us to struggle to succeed in living with Christ, when God says our new life has already been accomplished by Him. We are rich in Christ. We are free to lay hold of this wealth and live all the way up to the brim and beyond. "The just shall live by faith."[8] The question is not, "What can I have and when can I get it?" It is, rather, "What have I got and how do I live it?" All the fullness of God lives within you, if you know Christ, and He lives it in you as you simply trust Him.

At this moment I feel I must say something again about the church, the body of Christ. Jesus said, "For where two or three have gathered together in My name, there I am in their midst."[9] This is the church in its simplest form. The Holy Spirit has not been given first to the individual;

He has first been given to the church. This is not to say
we cannot experience His fullness as persons. Whatever is
true of the whole is true of the part. Since we are members, or cells, in the body of Christ, since He lives in the
entire body, He naturally indwells each cell. But the issue
is this: it is not so much a matter of how I as a person can
experience the reality of the Spirit, but rather how *we* as
a *body* can enjoy His presence. Invite God to lead you to
a group of people who meet together in a home or office
in the name of Jesus Christ. Hearing a speaker once each
week is fine, but it misses by a country mile what we are
after here. That may teach us *about* God, but we need
fellowship *with* Him, and He has so clearly indicated that
fellowship with Him comes best in a pluralistic scene. Else
why would He have admonished us to frequently assemble
ourselves together?[10]

Today, we have gotten away from this, but I believe God
is bringing us around again. The *body* needs to function,
not just a speaker within the body. We are accustomed to
the whole body being a mouth. God desires, for our benefit
and upbuilding, that all the members function.

In considering the element of time as related to the
Holy Spirit, the Scriptures often speak of our walk in the
Spirit. Our relationship with the Spirit of God operates on
a continuum. Just as it would be inconceivable for God to
pump the Holy Spirit in and out of the church, so it would
make little sense for the Spirit to be on-again, off-again
in our lives. It is interesting that Paul ascribes to the Lord
the role of supplier of the Spirit, or, literally, "He who keeps
on providing you with the Spirit."[11] It is God's job to keep
His Spirit coming our way; all He desires on our part is
that we rely upon Him to do so.

On the negative side, we often wonder if we quench or

grieve the Spirit, or if we sin, will the Spirit depart from us. I feel we must return at this point to the opening verse of Romans 8, where we began. Sin has been judged at the cross. Or later in that same chapter, when Paul writes:

32. He who did not spare His own Son, but delivered Him up for us all, how will He not also with Him freely give us all things?
33. Who will bring a charge against God's elect? God is the one who justifies;
34. who is the one who condemns? Christ Jesus is He who died, yes, rather who was raised, who is at the right hand of God, who also intercedes for us.
35. Who shall separate us from the love of Christ? Shall tribulation, or distress, or persecution, or famine, or nakedness, or peril, or sword?

God wants us off this introspection kick. He wants us to trust Him. As we depend on Him, for our forgiveness, for His love, for the provision of His Holy Spirit — not just alone, but with the fellowship of brothers and sisters in Christ — He will be real to us.

A child growing up can become a tragic personality cripple if he is constantly wondering if he has grieved his parents or if they are displeased with him. Part of the role of a mother and father is, because they love and adore him, to teach him what kind of person he should be and tell him how to live effectively.

So it is with God. If we have grieved or displeased Him, He will no doubt tap us on the shoulder and discipline (teach) us how to do it right. But it is *through* the Holy Spirit that He does this. That is a part of His leading in our lives. He does not give us over to ourselves the moment we spout off. He keeps us as His own.

We are educated by our superficial human, and even sometimes family, relationships to expect estrangement every time we do something wrong. If I lose a business deal, I expect the boss to be angry with me. If I make a poor showing in a classroom discussion, I am not surprised by a disappointed glare from my instructor. If I make a *faux pas* in high society, I can count on a cold shoulder from the elite. So naturally, when a person is tuned into the way the world runs, he expects God to withdraw from his presence if he sins.

I do not wish to sound like a broken record, but God says we're forgiven. We are accepted in the beloved. And in place of falsely counting on breaking fellowship with Him, let's start counting on the "grace of the Lord Jesus Christ, and the love of God, and the fellowship of the Holy Spirit . . . ."[12] (Paul wrote *that* to the gross Corinthians!)

God says we are new people. He has planted within us new life. Old life looks at sin; new life looks at forgiveness. Old life is in fear; new life is in love. Old life expects estrangement; new life thrives on fellowship with God. Let's forget once and for all this emphasis on performance living and conditioned love. It's time we learn to walk in confidence with God, expecting Him to use us, counting on Him to anoint us with power. If we should slip, let's trust the Saviour and keep moving. He's taken care of all that.

This is what the world is waiting to see. People want something that works. We've been lifted far above this "up and down" kind of existence. We're seated in the heavenlies. God calls us overcomers — still meeting the problems that life offers — but overcomers. Winners! And the Holy Spirit within is the One who makes this life possible.

Some Thoughts on Happiness

For who is our hope or joy or crown of exultation? Is it not even you, in the presence of our Lord Jesus at His coming? For you are our glory and joy.

I Thessalonians 2:19,20

11.

Some Thoughts on Happiness

The University of Iowa is beautifully situated on the green rolling hills that border the Iowa River, which flows directly through the campus. The students are typically Midwestern — warm and friendly.

During a recent trip to that school, I was talking with a freshman in the student union. He had become a Christian the previous fall and was growing rapidly in his new life.

"I really like this stuff I've been hearing on the love and grace of God," he said, as we sat down together over a Coke in the commons. "Right after I met the Lord, I got on this huge pressure binge of witnessing for Christ. I was told, either by words or inference, that it was necessary for my own growth, and that God would really be pleased with me if I witnessed regularly. Naturally I did.

153

"When I began to understand that God's love for me was based on something far deeper and more permanent, I began to know a freedom in my life that I had never experienced before. I felt liberated from *having* to witness to everyone and from the guilt that followed if I didn't. I have grown far more since that time than in all the rest of my Christian life put together.

"There's only one hang-up," he went on. "I'm still not completely happy. I love to see people trust in Jesus Christ, but since I've gotten off this pressure thing, I haven't shared my faith a whole lot. Last fall I saw some action in my outreach; this spring I'm more at peace in my own heart, but there's still something missing. Know what I mean?"

I knew what he meant. I had been through it. It happens sometimes when we have lived for an extended period of time under the dictates of law, and then all of a sudden break out into the pleasant atmosphere of God's grace. Rather than respond from within, we respond at the point of situation, and thus fail to see the total purpose of our activity.

At first, I was concerned as I saw this problem in my own experience and in the lives of others. But the cause for alarm has dwindled. After all, which is better — to walk by a program of forced works, or to live by the power of the Holy Spirit, even though some adjustments may be needed? I'll take the latter any day of the week. And if our new walk really *is* in the power of the Spirit, not only will there be ultimate good works which result, but just as important, the new works will be the real thing!

After a brief pause in the conversation, I looked up at my friend across the table. "What do you think it is that makes a free man genuinely happy?" I inquired, sensing that the Lord had given me that question to pose to him.

He looked puzzled. "I'm not really sure," he responded.

My thoughts started paging through notes and lectures filed away in the closets of my memory to come up with something impressive and theologically profound. Then God reminded me to keep it simple. Simple? I wasn't even sure of the answer myself! "God is our Father, and we're His sons," I thought. "Maybe we can go with the father-son idea on a human level and arrive at a spiritual parallel."

"Dave," I said, "in an earthly, human relationship, what is it that makes a father happy with reference to his son?"

"I suppose when the kid obeys him," he replied.

Still fishing for the answer myself, I shot back, "But what if the kid obeys him with a grudge?"

"Then that wouldn't make him happy," Dave reasoned.

"I *am* a father," I thought to myself. "What is it in relation to my kids that makes *me* happy?"

Earlier that day, while driving from Chicago to Iowa City, I had stopped at a filling station for gas. While I was waiting inside the building for the attendant to service my car, I spotted a rack of children's toys nearby. Even though I made mental note that these guys were robbers in the prices they were asking, my attention was drawn to a small, metal gyroscope displayed along with the other items. I could practically hear my kids squeal if they had a chance to see it work. The thought of my own childhood bewilderment at seeing a gyroscope spin on a string or a pencil point came to my mind. I knew it was way overpriced, but I decided to go ahead and get it anyway, just because it would make them happy.

I related the incident to Dave. "Isn't the thing that makes a father happy, the happiness of his children?" I asked.

"I guess it is," he replied slowly, still thinking the matter over in his mind.

"If that's true, and if the analogy holds," I said, "it must mean that God is happy when we are happy."

We both stopped talking and were silent. That seemed too simple. Sometimes, I think, we are so accustomed to the Word of God being presented negatively that when a bit of good news comes through to us, we tend to reject it and think, "Naw, God couldn't be *that* good." The thing we miss is that He is the actual *source* of goodness itself. How could man's standard for good ever be higher than His?

Part of the reason Jesus came to this planet was to give us true happiness. "These things I have spoken to you," Jesus said, "that My joy may be in you, and that your joy may be made full."[1] He wants us to be happy. And it gave Him great joy to be the one who cleansed us from sin. "Fixing our eyes on Jesus the author and perfecter of faith, who for the joy set before Him endured the cross . . . ."[2] Jesus Christ possessed great joy in dying for us, knowing that in the end, our happiness would be complete. The thing that makes God happy is when we're happy, and the thing that makes us happy is knowing that God loves us and has completely forgiven us.

So often, happiness is a memory of the past or a hope for the future. Many times we hear people express themselves whose basic attitude toward life is, "I wish the Lord would take me home." Or, just today someone said, "If only I could have lived in the times of Jesus." But what about *right now?* God loves you *now.* If your life were to improve 100% every day for the rest of your life, His love for you wouldn't increase one bit. God has given to you right now every ounce of love He possibly has in His possession.

It is yours. And it gives God great joy to know that you and I are experiencing His joy, a product of His love.

Now, if God is happy when we are happy, it would also follow that we will be most happy when we make others happy. So much of love is in giving. "By this the love of God was manifested in us, that God has sent His only begotten Son into the world so that we might live through Him."[3]

I have been tempted all my life to try to manipulate people. One writer put it this way: "God created us to love people and use things; our problem comes in loving things and using people." It was partly through realization of this vanity on my part that I came to trust in Christ. I had tried loving others in my own strength, and my strength gave out! I know of nothing that provides the human soul with more emptiness and frustration than the aftermath of exploitation. I think back to incidents in my own life when I was forced to live with myself after taking selfish advantage of another person. I would invariably, upon these occasions, ask myself, "Why did you do it?" but would never emerge with any answers. Even though I may have gained materially or egotistically through these incidents, I never came away happy.

What a contrast to living in the life and love of Jesus Christ. Instead of looking for ways others can benefit me, I am now free to look for ways I can benefit others. And in the life of love, you often do not get your way — but a heart of giving *does* make you happy. I guess that's why St. Francis in understanding God's love for him could write:[4]

> Lord, make me an instrument of Thy peace.
> Where there is hatred let me sow love;
> Where there is injury, pardon;

Where there is doubt, faith;
Where there is despair, hope;
Where there is darkness, light;
Where there is sadness, joy.

O Divine Master, grant that I may not so much seek
To be consoled as to console;
To be understood as to understand;
To be loved as to love;
For it is in giving that we receive;
It is in pardoning that we are pardoned;
It is in dying that we are born to eternal life.

Now, if it is through Jesus Christ that I can be made happy, it would stand to reason that other people would be happy, too, knowing God loves and has forgiven them. In other words, since God is pleased when I am happy, and I am pleased when making others happy, the best way in all the world to allow others our kind of joy is to introduce them to Jesus Christ. John said as he wrote his first epistle, "And these things we write, so that our joy may be made complete."[5] Just having a chance to spread the good news about Jesus Christ gave John great joy. It made his joy complete. I like to call it running the "joy-cycle." Every time we have the opportunity in *any* way to relate the love of God to others, our joy-cycle gets completed and fulfilled all over again.

It was that same week in Iowa that I was speaking in a fraternity house one evening to a group of men and women from the University. As I was describing the love of God, I spotted a girl near the front of the group who seemed especially attentive. She seemed to hang on everything that was being said, and I knew that God was conversing with her. After the meeting concluded, she was the first one to come up to me and talk. She introduced herself and said, "You will never know how much that helped me tonight."

"You accepted Jesus Christ tonight, didn't you?" I said.

Tears came into her eyes. "Yes, I did, a-and I'm s-s-so happy!" she blurted out.

I don't cry easily, but I became a bit choked up myself. "That makes me happy, too," I said enthusiastically.

And it really *did!*

But witnessing for Christ isn't always the big deal we seem to make it — it's part of *life.* Very little is said in the New Testament with regard to firm commands to "get the word out." /Salvation just happened. When you are in love, it's the natural thing to talk about it. Jesus did not say, "you must"; He said, "you shall."[6] Peter told a group of elders, "Shepherd the flock of God among you, not under compulsion, but voluntarily . . . ."[7]

A friend we have known for years is a business executive in Chicago. When he hires new management men for his firm, he brings in an industrial psychologist to help him screen his applicants. They will generally set aside several hours during a specific week for the appointments, and my friend sits in on these sessions to observe and evaluate while the consultant conducts the interview.

"We had men scheduled at different times all week," he told me. "I have never experienced a series of interviews like it."

When the first man was brought into his office, he said, the professional interviewer made sure the applicant was comfortably seated, and after introductions and appropriate greetings, the questioning began.

"He started out with all the easy ones like — where are

you from? — married? — how many children? — what is your educational background? — until the guy was pretty near asleep. Then just as the man being interviewed was becoming confident, the consultant asked him, as if out of the blue, 'What is your purpose in life?' "

My friend described how the applicant was caught off guard and really had no answer. The interview, for all practical purposes, had terminated.

This technique of questioning continued all week. After each man was ushered in and seated in an easy chair, the opening questions would flow smoothly and the answers would come easily. Then, as the men would begin to relax, the target question would be posed.

Finally, as the week wore on, the last of the scheduled appointments arrived. As with the rest, he was introduced, warmly welcomed, and the interview was under way. After ten minutes or so of the easy questions, out it came.

"What is your purpose in life," the interviewer demanded.

With hardly a moment's hesitation the man replied, "My purpose in life is to have eternal life and to take as many people with me as possible!"

This time, too, the interview, for all practical purposes, was ended. The one conducting the questions was so caught by surprise, that he had few questions left to ask.

Here was a man in the business world, not being paid to say one word about spiritual life, and yet one who expressed a reason to live which far outstripped the man who was the seeming expert on how to live!

If our Christianity is a programmed set of rules and activities, we are certain candidates for spiritual fatigue and waning interest. But if we catch the life of Christ as it really is, knowing Him becomes more creative and rewarding each day. It is the experience with a God who shows up, and who is there continually with a compassion and concern that never stops. It is Jesus living in us, and we in Him, in a relationship without fear of threat or termination.

Love Is Now

Behold, I will do a new thing; now it shall spring forth....

Isaiah 43:19

12.

Love Is Now

The thought has come to mind at times, "Do I really *understand* completely all these things about God's love and grace?" Over and over again, my assurance has been that regardless of whether or not I understand analytically, I am *in* His love and His grace because I am in Him. God Himself says that His love is beyond intellectual comprehension;[1] the amazing thing is that because of Jesus Christ His love is wonderfully within the possession range of our experience.

A great and subtle tendency for me is to attempt to grow in truth, doctrine, and methods, and not to grow in Jesus Christ. A system of thought is a much more convenient method of understanding, a far more natural atmosphere to our human life, than is the Person of Christ Himself. For

it is He who is our life, not our objective and "pure" understanding of Him. It is He who lives, not words about Him.
". . . The letter kills, but the Spirit gives life."[2]
In my own experience, I needed to know that all my
sins were forgiven at Calvary, once-for-all, because an in-
complete awareness of God's forgiveness kept me shielded
from a receptive and living confidence before Him. Knowing the love of God has changed my very being because
knowing His love has allowed me to accept myself, others,
and even Him in a brand-new way. Knowing my freedom
in Jesus has permitted me an escape from the limitations
of old, mechanical motions that have always been such an
integral part of my life and perspective.

I see myself no longer as a machine of God, but as a
man of God. He is not interested in me first as a vessel
or an instrument, but as a person. Therefore, when He says
that He fills me with the Holy Spirit, I see a real-life individual as the possessor of that Spirit, and not an impersonal conduit. His Spirit is not within like the blinking
light of a neon sign, on-again and off-again; He is instead
in me as *life*. By His matchless Holy Spirit I am wed to
Him and to the body of His Son in a living way, a way
that lasts and is permanent and consistent in His life.

His Spirit does not yank and pull itself from me only
to return again to potentially depart, anymore than I would
continually divorce myself from my wife but keep on coming back for more. That is not relationship; it is reaction.
Love *acts* rather than *reacts*. God is active in our behalf,
and He has taken up residence in the hearts of all who
welcome Him.

The reason that forgiveness, undemanding love, freedom,
and all the rest have made such a personal impact is that
through the new vision of these manifestations of Jesus

Christ the debris of legalism, fear, self-condemnation, and formula-living has been swept aside and discarded. In a sense I have begun all over again to be unencumbered by religion, to know Jesus Christ as I did when I began with Him ten years ago. My goal is not to garner new insights into forgiveness as such; it is to know Him. I do not wish to pursue the theological intricacies of how freedom works, or to apply new principles to the ministry of the Holy Spirit so that I may better contain Him. My desire is Jesus Christ Himself.

In responding to the power of Simon Peter's life the religious authorities did not say they felt He knew a lot about Jesus, for they had already perceived Peter and his cohorts were ignorant and unlearned men. They saw that these men had been *with* Jesus.[3] He was a very part of them. People did not approach the apostles and say, "We desire to grasp more fully the teachings of your Saviour." They said to Philip, "Sir, we wish to see Jesus."[4] Facts about "light" are not the issue for, "In Him was life; and the life was the light of men."[5]

God craves us for Himself at whatever point we may be at this instant! He loves us right now. Love is now because God is now. He is not waiting for us to change — He will perform the changes. He will not tarry for lack of understanding, for He brings with Him understanding. He wants to impart *Himself* to us. And He wants to do it *now*.

Jesus is our life. *Nothing* need be accomplished to make Him more available to us than He is right now. No promises, no factual data, no deprivations, no amends. These have all been borne by Him, and He is life itself. Out of Him, out of His life in us, will come our lives. Because He is, we are. As I trust Him on a "this moment" basis, His presence and His love will be manifest in me, for me, and to me. It is this life which, in turn, will produce the reality of Christ to others.

There is another tendency I find in my life pattern that limits the thrust of our God. And that is to turn to the Scriptures, to prayer, and to the Word alone. *Alone.* There is no more empty word in my vocabulary than *alone.* Certainly, I will learn of Him and feast upon His love in the silence and solitude of my private chambers. As we spend quiet hours together in secret, He will unveil Himself to me in a new array of loveliness.

But it is in His body where Jesus dwells. That was true during His physical life on earth, and it is equally true of His spiritual life on earth. And by spiritual, I do not mean an ethereal, make-believe life. I mean the life He lives in us today through the Holy Spirit. God's Spirit has been sent to the church, the body, and not as "many" Holy Spirits to individual upon individual. We know and experience the Lord Jesus best as we know Him through His body.

If you receive a picture and a letter from a new acquaintance, you can know him on a limited basis that way. But seeing him in person and being with him allow you a far greater opportunity for fellowship and unity.

Jesus is best known in person. Since it may be awhile before we go to Him, He has agreed to come to us. He is present today in His body. Most people are! But His body is different, in that sense, from our own. We possess individual bodies; His body is corporate. It is composed of all who trust Him. And you and I will never know optimal oneness with Him in this life unless we know oneness with Him through others.

Do you tire of being a loner spiritually, as I do? I pray that you do. His love right now is ours through something far beyond our personal relationship with Him. His love is ours through a corporate relationship with Him as well.

What can we do? There are no rules. It is the Holy Spirit who rules. Love makes us vulnerable. And openness to others within the body is often new because we are so used to being alone. Or we are so accustomed to coming together to share with others world-type things *only*. Or we simply report to one another that which He is doing with us and for us and not what He *is* to us. There is nothing wrong with issues and works that we see as a result of His presence. But it is He Himself who is the foundation of our oneness. Jesus is our life together.

I cannot tell you what to do. We are too "do" oriented as it is. Just follow the Lamb wherever He goes. Trust yourself to the Fulfiller of your heart's desires. And as His life is ministered to you, He will doubtless begin, if He has not already begun, to draw you together in fellowship and intra-personal oneness with those of like precious faith. *Where* this happens is not the issue. Why not just let it happen? As you depend on Him alone, you will find this life with others sooner than you think, for God is God *right now*. And His love is that way, too.

Finally, whether we like to admit it or not, we lean toward becoming products of our environment. That is one reason Paul told the Romans, "Do not be conformed to this world,"[6] or as J. B. Phillips translates it, "Don't let the world around you squeeze you into its own mould . . . ."[7] Ours is an age of specialization. In formal education we are learning more and more about less and less. From its industrial beginnings, for example, the automobile has evolved from a "horseless carriage" to a complex transport device. No longer capable of being serviced just by a mechanic, we now need transmission specialists, front end specialists, and another whole new team to repair the air conditioner. In the same way, we rarely employ one group of men to build a home. Today we contract separately for the plumber, the electrician, the interior designer, and on and on.

This same philosophy of specialization has carried over into the spiritual realm as well. In the beginning there was the church. Today there is the church, plus. We have training centers or seminaries, evangelistic organizations, welfare agencies, Christian political movements, and even people who write Christian books!

A result of this spiritual smorgasbord of available goods and services is that each one pushes "his own thing." Each group emphasizes its own distinctive or specialty. And unfortunately the whole business comes through to us in such a way that we begin to think that unless we have tasted a portion of what each specialty house has to offer, there is no way to enjoy victory in the Christian life. By implication, joy with Christ is always another Bible conference, Christian book, or theological insight away.

The "soul-winner" says that until we master his technique and give our lives to witnessing, we will be unfulfilled. The "personal devotions" proponent says that the deepening of one's life in the Word is the final answer to personal need. Renewal comes, says the specialist in "small groups," when people come together in the environment of honesty and quest. One who has experienced a "spiritual gift" claims a new dimension of depth and satisfaction, and often views others as missing out unless they obtain his gift.

Where does God fit into all of this? And how does Joe Christian come to know the simplicity of the person of Jesus Christ when, just as he thinks he's found the final missing link to his faith, somebody else comes along and says, "Here, try my shortcut."

Not only is God in love with us where we are, but He wants us to be in love with Him where He is, too. Certainly, if you or I need something further in our Christian experience, we can trust Him (if we can trust *anybody*) to give it to us, and more. "If you then, being evil, know how to give good gifts to your children, how much more shall your Father who is in heaven give what is good to those who ask Him!" [8] Jesus Christ will not withhold ever from us one single thing that we need to have victory in Him.

Men and movements, yes, even those who write books, will tell you they have the secret to victory and joy in Christ. Make sure when you listen that the "secret" is Jesus and not another activity, law, goal, strategy, or something else. Imagine the Apostle Paul coming along with a line like this: "Until you've experienced all that I have experienced, there is no way to enjoy a consistent Christian life." Could *any* of us ever have a chance to experience all that he had seen and heard and done? Experiences come from Jesus Christ; Jesus Christ does not come from experiences. It is He who is our experience, author and perfecter of our faith.

"As you therefore have received Christ Jesus the Lord, so walk in Him, having been firmly rooted and now being built up in Him and established in your faith . . . ." [9] We are *now being* built up in Him. The Lord is our Shepherd; we shall not want. And He loves us now, for love is now, and God is love!

NOTES

CHAPTER 1

[1] John 10:10(KJV).
[2] George Whitefield, *Journals* (London: Banner of Truth, 1960), p. 209.

CHAPTER 2

[1] Ephesians 2:8-10.
[2] I Corinthians 15:3.
[3] Hebrews 10:10; Ephesians 1:7; Romans 4:7, 8.
[4] Isaiah 55:8, 9.
[5] Romans 8:1, 2; Romans 6:22; II Corinthians 5:17.
[6] Micah 7:19.
[7] Psalm 103:12.
[8] Isaiah 44:22.
[9] James 2:10.
[10] Romans 8:1.
[11] Hebrews 6:10.
[12] II Peter 1:9.
[13] Luke 7:48.

CHAPTER 3

[1] Romans 5:8.
[2] I am using the account in Luke 7:36-50.
[3] Luke 7:40-42.
[4] I Samuel 16:7.
[5] Luke 7:44-46.
[6] Proverbs 7:17.
[7] Luke 7:47.
[8] S. I. McMillen, *None of These Diseases* (Westwood: Fleming H. Revell, 1963), p. 116.
[9] Ezekiel 18:4.
[10] Romans 6:23.
[11] I Peter 1:16 (KJV).

[12] Jude 24; Colossians 1:22.
[13] Compare Genesis 22:8 with John 1:29.
[14] Micah 7:18.

CHAPTER 4

[1] For a clear discussion of gnosticism, see *The International Standard Bible Encyclopaedia*, Volume II (Grand Rapids: Eerdmans, 1939), pp. 1240-1248.
[2] Ephesians 5:8.
[3] I John 4:18.
[4] John 16:9.
[5] I John 2:12.

CHAPTER 5

[1] I John 4:19 (KJV).
[2] Ephesians 4:15.
[3] Romans 5:7, 8.
[4] Isaiah 59:2.
[5] Hebrews 9:7.
[6] I John 4:18.

CHAPTER 6

[1] Romans 2:4.
[2] Luke 15:11-32.
[3] Luke 15:20.
[4] John 5:24.
[5] John 19:30.
[6] John 3:36.
[7] II Corinthians 5:19.
[8] Psalms 32:1, 2; 130:3.
[9] Hebrews 8:12.
[10] Philippians 4:13.
[11] II Peter 1:3.
[12] Hebrews 13:5.

CHAPTER 7

[1] I John 4:19.
[2] Mark 12:31.
[3] Ephesians 5:28.

⁴ II Timothy 2:21.
⁵ I Corinthians 6:11.
⁶ Revelation 1:6.
⁷ Ephesians 2:10.

CHAPTER 8

¹ Acts 13:44.
² Acts 17:6.
³ Acts 5:13.
⁴ Romans 6:2.
⁵ Colossians 3:14.
⁶ II Corinthians 5:17.
⁷ Matthew 7:1.
⁸ Romans 14:1.
⁹ John 15:19.
¹⁰ *Ibid.*
¹¹ *Ibid.*
¹² John 17:14.
¹³ I Timothy 5:8.
¹⁴ Notice the plural pronouns in such passages as Ephesians 4: 13, 15, 16, and I Corinthians 12:18-24.
¹⁵ I Corinthians 14:26 sounds very similar to this.
¹⁶ Matthew 16:18 (KJV).
¹⁷ Acts 2:47.
¹⁸ See I Corinthians 5:1–6:11.
¹⁹ To be removed from the church is to be placed back in the world, and "the whole world lies in the power of the evil one" (I John 5:19).
²⁰ Hebrews 12:6.
²¹ II Corinthians 2:6-10.
²² "Until the latter part of the second century . . . meetings were held secretly in private houses. During the third century many 'Lord's houses' or 'churches' were erected, and considerable attention was given, in the wealthier communities, to architecture and to internal decoration" (A. H. Newman, *A Manual of Church History,* Volume I [Philadelphia: Judson Press, 1933], p. 295).
²³ "Christian churches assumed the magnificence of heathen temples. In imitating the pomp, Christians were sure to imi-

tate the practices of heathenism, especially as the most influ-
ential Christians were now men that had been brought up
pagans, and had adopted Christianity chiefly because it was
the fashion" (*Ibid.*, p. 313).
24 It is interesting that the trend toward "church in the home"
has even influenced the President! During the early months
of his administration, Mr. Nixon has often been worshiping
on Sunday mornings with a group of friends in the White
House.
25 See Philemon 8-10.
26 Matthew 16:18.

CHAPTER 9

1 Hebrews 8:13.
2 Hebrews 8:10.
3 I Corinthians 15:56.
4 Galatians 3:24.
5 Psalm 37:4.
6 John 10:10.
7 John 8:32.
8 II Corinthians 3:17.

Chapter 10

1 Galatians 3:2.
2 Jeremiah 31:33.
3 Matthew 5:44.
4 Matthew 6:14.
5 James 1:2-4.
6 I John 2:1.
7 John 3:34.
8 Romans 1:17 (KJV).
9 Matthew 18:20.
10 Hebrews 10:25.
11 Galatians 3:5.
12 II Corinthians 13:14.

CHAPTER 11

1 John 15:11.
2 Hebrews 12:2.

[3] I John 4:9.
[4] This is the famous "Prayer of St. Francis," and is found, among other places, in Maria Sticco, *The Peace of St. Francis* (New York: Hawthorne Books, Inc., 1962), p. 285.
[5] I John 1:4.
[6] Acts 1:8.
[7] I Peter 5:2.

CHAPTER 12

[1] Ephesians 3:19.
[2] II Corinthians 3:6.
[3] Acts 4:13.
[4] John 12:21.
[5] John 1:4.
[6] Romans 12:2.
[7] J. B. Phillips, *The New Testament in Modern English* (New York: Macmillan, 1959), p. 332.
[8] Matthew 7:11.
[9] Colossians 2:6, 7.